OLE BERT

SAGE OF THE SMOKIES

BY

H.C. "WOODY" BRINEGAR

THIRD EDITION

THIS EDITION PUBLISHED BY
BLOUNT COUNTY LIBRARY
FRIENDS OF THE LIBRARY
2019

Table of Contents

PREFACE TO THE THIRD EDITION

Mountains inspire a different kind of thinking, sometimes fanciful sometimes profound. A mountain range is an odd place, especially to those who grow up or are accustomed to the plains and even for those who are used to hills and valleys. The mountains are magical, and you can't help but feel that they are hiding some secrets just as they hide the sun during normal times of sunshine.

That mystery is evident even for those who live in or near mountains. The mountains draw us in and invite us to see and hear the world with different eyes and ears–just as the topography tells us that there is something different about the world we are experiencing.

Mountains threaten and comfort us at the same time. They challenge our received logic, and they offer us the beauty of nature that is found nowhere else.

Bert Garner, sage of the Smokies, understood all of this at some deep level. He loved the Great Smoky Mountains and spent much of his life exploring their aspects and discovering their secrets. "If there are no mountains in Heaven, let me go sommers else," he wrote. "These mountains are stately epics of the Almighty, where I have always found a ready grave for my sorrows."

Bert Garner was a true mountain man–not just in the Jeremiah Johnson sense, although he could boast of plenty of experiences in that regard. Ole Bert invited the mountains to be part of his thinking, part of his spirit, and ultimately part of his soul. To him, the mountains had a simplicity of appearance and a complexity of purpose. Garner ordered his life in this way–a simplicity of lifestyle and a complexity of purpose.

Those of us who love the mountains, especially the Great Smoky Mountains, are indebted to Bert for what he learned and what he tried to teach us by his writing, his conversation, and the conduct of his life.

We are also indebted to Woody Brinegar, who put his friendship with Bert to good use by producing this remembrance and record of some of the words and actions of this most interesting and unique character.

The Blount County Friends of the Library is happy to bring out this third edition of Woody's work–an edition we hope will extend Bert's reach out from the mountains and across hills, valleys, and plains to future generations of mountain lovers. The editors would like to thank Lisa Misosky and Andy Lombardo for their generosity in allowing us to use the files that they had set up for the second edition.

Special thanks is due to Brennan LeQuire who proofread the book and made many helpful suggestions.

All of the proceeds of this book will go to the Blount County Friends of the Library. More about that organization can be found at the back of the book.

Jim Stovall

SECOND EDITION INFORMATION

Ole Bert: Sage of the Smokies

by

H.C. (Woody) Brinegar

Original Text Copyright © 1982 by Woody Brinegar

Second edition: Reprinted in 2009 by

'27/'37 Publishing

with Permission of the Brinegar Family

Book design by

Andy Lombardo

PUBLISHER'S NOTE TO THE SECOND EDITION

It has long been a desire of ours to bring *Ole Bert, Sage of the Smokies* back into print. By any account, it enjoyed a too short life in print, originally printed and self-distributed by Woody Brinegar in 1982. It is very seldom that one comes across a copy of *Ole Bert*, and, considering the world today, Bert's observations are more prophetic and poignant today than ever before.

It is our distinct pleasure to offer this publication with the blessings of the Brinegar family. Although Ole Bert considered that there were already too many publications cluttering up the world, we think he'd approve of this volume (the second edition) on a very practical level, because a portion of the sale of each book will be to two charitable.

We hope that you enjoy sitting down and having a visit with Ole Bert. Although you can no longer sit and stay a spell with the man described as "more Thoreau than Thoreau himself," this volume should give you a taste of the ideas and viewpoints of the Sage of the Smokies.

With pleasure,
'27/'37 Publishing (2009)

DEDICATION

Dedicated to Libby Brinegar,

Woody's biggest supporter and fan

PREFACE TO THE SECOND EDITION

We are pleased that our father's book *Ole Bert* is being published again so that many more readers can enjoy it.

Daddy loved Bert Garner, philosophy, turning a fine phrase, and nature, especially the mountains. He was able to combine those interests in this one project.

Many of you over the years have wanted to get a copy of dad's book and now it's possible.

I, Lisa, remember helping him edit the book in the summer of '73, right after my freshman year in college.

My sister and I hope this endeavor will help keep the spirit and name of our father alive. He was truly a larger than life character and deserves to be remembered.

We would like to dedicate this book to the memory of our beloved mother Libby Brinegar who was dad's biggest supporter and fan.

She would have loved to see dad's book available to a whole new generation and to those who did not get a copy of the first edition.

Our thanks go to Southland Books, Lisa Misosky, Andy Lombardo, and others who made this book possible. The entire endeavor has had the blessing of the Brinegar family since the very beginning.

It is our hope that my father's words enrich your lives as they did ours.

Woody's daughters

Lisa Brinegar Slagle

Barbara Brinegar Burgess

Knoxville TN

July 17, 2008

INTRODUCTION

Herbert S. Garner, or Ole Bert as he insisted on being called, was one of nature's oddlings. A remarkably interesting and refreshing personality was this aberration. He came to my attention through a number of articles over a period of time in the Maryville and Knoxville newspapers. Several of these were in reference to his appearance on The Garry Moore Television Show in New York in January, 1957. Two columns were written by Hal Boyle, syndicated columnist and Pulitzer Prize winner. Others were by local journalists.

The articles stressed the simple life he lived in a cabin near Maryville, his broad range of interests, his large library, his habit of walking, and his affinity to the mountains. They depicted a charming and delightful man, gray, weathered, traveled, and companionable, walking a divergent path from his fellows, a modern day Thoreau.

It was in April 1967, that I met Ole Bert on a hike to Gregory Bald, on the western end of the Great Smoky Mountains. Paul Bales, a mutual friend, had arranged the outing, and Bert Garner was one of the party.

No one in the group relished the eleven mile walk as much as Bert who was 81 at the time. His presence heightened immeasurably the enjoyment of all. To walk and talk with him added a different dimension to any journey.

I normally keep notes of my mountain walks, and these record some of the topics which were discussed. He talked of books on the Smokies including Horace

Kephart's *Our Southern Highlanders*, which is recognized as a major work on the character of the mountain people. Bert told of meeting Kephart on Gregory in 1907 and his impressions of him. They had camped together at Moore's Spring. Kephart had a mule to pack in his camping gear Sage of the Smokies and had commented that Bert traveled like an Indian with his rolled blanket and knapsack. Said Bert, "Kephart was an excellent cook, and was equipped with everything from A to Z. His book, *Camping and Woodcraft*, was in print until recently." Bert spoke of *The Travels of William Bartram*, Bartram's published record of his travel experiences in the southeast beginning in 1773, searching for botanical specimens. One discovery was the flame azalea which blooms on Gregory in June. I got an inkling of Bert's phenomenal memory when I checked upon my return and found that he had quoted nearly verbatim Bartram's description of the flame or fiery azalea.

"The epithet fiery I annex to this most celebrated species of azalea, as being expressive of the appearance of its flowers; which are in general of the color of the finest red lead, orange, and bright gold, as well as yellow and cream color. This is certainly the most gay and brilliant flowering shrub yet known." Bert told of visiting Bartram's Botanical Gardens in Philadelphia on several occasions.

At lunch on top of the bald, resting in lush grass beneath a serviceberry tree, we got into our sandwiches, canned meat, sodas, and so on. Bert took a small paper bag and a paper cup from his satchel, poured the cup about half full with a light brown powdery concoction, filled it with water, stirred it with a twig, and began to drink. When asked what he was going to eat, he answered, "I am eating. This is my normal repast when on the trail."

"What is it?"

"It's ground wheat and soybeans mixed with chocolate. I can carry a week's supply in less space than you use for your lunch. In fact, I can put a day's needs in one pocket. I figure my lunch costs less than a nickel. What about yours, Paul?"

Paul answered with, "I don't know, but this Pepsi cost twelve cents, and I brought three of them."

While taking a break on the way down, the conversation touched on a local businessman. Stories were exchanged about some of his business dealings. Someone asked Bert what he thought of the man. His reply: "He's so crooked that when he dies Sam McCammon and Tom Click (morticians) will have to screw him into the ground," broke up the conversation and the rest stop.

We talked of chestnuts, whose imposing remains in the form of gray logs were in evidence along the path. I mentioned that Laura Thornborough in her book, *The Great Smoky Mountains*, had written of a hollow chestnut tree large enough to be used as a cow stall on a farm near Gatlinburg.

Bert recalled a November hike to Gregory Bald with neighbor Ike Razor thirty-five or so years ago. They began the twenty or so mile walk in pleasant fall weather and were hit by a snow storm the next day, a few miles short of the goal. "We holed up for two days in a hollow chestnut log in which I could stand

straight; so it was more than six feet on the inside."
We asked if they continued to the Bald, "No, we
weren't dressed for the weather and hoofed it home as
soon as the storm broke." His first trip to Gregory, he
said, was on horseback with his father and mother
when he was two and that he had returned more than
a hundred times over the years.

He talked of conservation, the population explosion, of
time and space, the question of how mountain balds
were formed and other matters. He appeared to be a
walking, talking encyclopedia, and we made plans for
another trip.

Before his death in August 1970, he gave me his
journals, covering the period from 1922 to 1970. From
these and our walks and talks and from conversations
with some of his friends comes the body of this work.
The purpose is to record something of Ole Bert, to view
some of the many sides of the man, to look at the
facade and to explore something of the essence of this
oddling. It is recognized that there are many facets of
his personality not touched on here and many shades
of him that the writer never saw.

My acquaintance at the end of his life left much of the
developing body of him beyond my view. His
companionship was one of life's delights to each of his
host of friends. As I got to know him, the enigma of the
man sharpened. The contrast in what I learned and
didn't know widened.

Rather than an integrated whole, this is a series of
essays and topics written between 1968 and 1975. It is
an arrangement of various materials concerning Ole

Bert. It is integrated only in that all topics deal with some of the many characteristics of the man.

It is my wish that these selections serve to rekindle some of that pleasure one always experienced in a visit with Ole Bert.

H. C. "Woody" Brinegar

September 1, 1982

Haywood Cumbie Brinegar
May 7, 1923 – March 25, 1995

Woody Brinegar lived for another quarter of a century after Bert Garner died. His love of the mountains grew during that time, and so did his standing in the community.

Woody was the head of the J.C. Gillespie Insurance Agency for a number of years and was well-known in the Maryville area as a civic leader and an advocate of the Great Smoky Mountains. He purchased a 60-acre farm in West Miller's Cove and at least two other mountain tracts. He would often retreat to those places to plant trees, clear out brush, and hike.

His expertise about the mountains and the plants and animals that lived there made him a valuable resource to the area. He wrote a column for the *Maryville-Alcoa Daily Times* on hiking.

It was in the mountains that Woody died, though the circumstances surrounding his death were tragic. He was found in his burning vehicle in West Miller's Cove after it had apparently veered off the road and slammed into a gate on his property. Woody had suffered from diabetes, and friends said that he had been having blackout spells. It is possible that one of these occurred while he was driving that day.

At his death, an editorial in the *Maryville-Alcoa Daily Times* called him "reflective and knowledgeable of the Smokies and the plants and animals who inhabited them." His life had "enriched the lives of many," the editorial concluded.

PARADISE (1969)

"**I** did better than old Elijah," he said, "I went to Heaven alive without a whirlwind. Here, where I live, is Paradise." Bert lived on the south slope of Needmore Hill southwest of Maryville in the undulating countryside of East Tennessee. The rolling land sweeps southward into Woodpecker Knobs, rising to Little Mountain nestled next to Chilhowee, and past Chilhowee on into the 'back of the beyond' of the big Smoky Mountains. In the winter's sun the peaks of LeConte and Gregory often shine as lofty jewels in hoarfrost or snow. The beckoning backbone of the Smokies outlines the horizon sweeping eastward. These hills and mountains form the backdrop of Bert Garner's Garden of Eden.

The pathway into Paradise begins on Needmore Road (Bert Garner Drive) and goes through Hugh Young's woods and past for three quarters of a mile from mailbox to cabin. In the foyer of the forest-crowned path, twin gray chestnut skeletons lean heavily against neighboring oaks. A strong breeze hurries the clouds eastward and sways the leaves into rustling song. Sunbeams slip through infrequent canopy openings, splashing bright irregular patches of light in the shaded hallway where the carpet of leaves and pine needles has been ground into bits by foot traffic.

A colorful towhee moves ahead in the trail, flies into a dogwood, and disappears into the undergrowth. The sharp cry of a blue jay heralds my approach. The walls of field pines are laced with dogwood and honeysuckle. The first fence across the way is of split chestnut rails dating back more than a hundred years. A small mulberry is heavy with green fruit.

I step into the open to cross the Aluminum Company power line right-of-way; two quail spring from beside the track in boisterous flight. The Chilhowee Mountains are prominent, their colors change with each variance of the sun and cloud cover, and with each atmospheric difference. From the mountainside leers the grotesque scar of the Happy Valley Road.

The last leg of the journey is beneath tall pines. Chestnut trunks lay in stately repose on the forest floor. A log by the barbed wire fence eases the crossing into Bert's Paradise.

Purple-stemmed raspberry bushes, fire pinks, Solomon's seal, spikenard, columbines, and irises grow in the clearing.

The siding of the cabin is weathered gray oak shingles. A screened porch is off the kitchen. Two down-sloping branches of a gnarled post oak brush against the asphalt shingle roof. A stately poplar and a beautiful hemlock stand in front. A serviceberry graces the right front corner. Ivy, Virginia creeper, and ground myrtle fight a thick battle for survival in this untended garden. The weather-beaten shack remains sound after fifty years and nestles snugly in the clearing, closed off from all outside except for a patch of sky.

A worn, penciled cardboard sign is stuck in the screen door, "UP IN THE WOODS. BACK SOON."

The fragrance of raw nature prevails. I marvel at Bert's having kept his Paradise unblemished for half a century. It is as restful, as enchanting, and as unusual as the ole man himself. The essence of the setting and of Bert is the same—natural and tranquil.

Bert comes around the cabin corner, "Hey you old reprobate, how be ye?" Until he got into a serious vein, his conversation was replete with colloquialisms.

"Fine, and you?"

"This sunshine is the finest medicine I've ever had. It's the best of physicians and cures more ills than a ton of pills."

"Didn't know you took pills."

"Never did till last year when they sheared my balls. Have taken a few aspirin since." (In the fall of 1968 he was operated on for cancer of the prostate.)

Bert stood tall, straight, and lean as a poplar sapling. His lively face was scored by the years giving the appearance of well-worn leather. Age hadn't bent him, and he looked younger than his eighty-three years.

"You're a walking, talking relic."

"Some say I'm a fossil, but only my head has turned to stone. Like the feller said, 'I aim to live to a hundred or die trying.'"

"Who tagged you the Sage of the Smokies? "

"Hal Boyle used it in one of his columns and maybe others, but I don't claim the title. It's a bit too imposing and conjures up much more than I am. 'Wild Sage' would be more accurate, for I have loved to sun and romp and sleep in fields of golden sage since a child. It is free as the wind, and in that sense only I am sage, broom sage."

"What about a tour of your place?" I asked.

"All right. We'll begin with my plumbing." We walked to the cistern immediately behind the porch.

"Now this is filled by putting that piece of guttering under the spout there and waiting for a good rain. There's a charcoal filter to cleanse out any debris from the roof. Crossing over to the woods on the west side, "My bath is a bit more rustic." From a cross pole between two pines hangs a rusty five gallon bucket with nail holes in the bottom.

"I step on this stump, pour the water in, step down, and bathe to my heart's content."

We walked to the far end of the clearing and into the woods a few paces and saw a broken-handled spade stuck in the ground.

"I dig a little trench here and after doing my business, cover it with a shovel or two of dirt. No trouble a'tall, sanitary and convenient.

"You know, the County Health man came out a year or so back. I believe he came to have me put in a septic field, but after he looked over my place including slit trench, shower and cistern, he shook his head and said, 'I didn't believe it till I saw it.' Anyhow, he said that for my purpose what I had was adequate."

"You're rather attached here, aren't you?"

"I'm planted in these woods as deeply as the roots of my trees," he answered.

The woodshed, called his summer house, is about 200 feet in front of the cabin closed off by intervening trees. It's a tall, gray, frame building twelve by thirteen feet, with a small loft. Inside is a stack of stove wood, fruit jars once used for canning, odd garden tools, and bits of string and rope hanging from nails, and a small hand grinder fastened to the end of a standing log.

"What's that?"

"I use it to grind my corn for cornbread and for wheat and soybeans. When hiking or when fresh food was scarce, I used to live off ground wheat and soybeans. There is always something green available, water cress or dandelion."

5

He climbed up the wooden ladder to the loft and filled one of his coat pockets with walnuts from a wooden keg, saying, "While we're here, I'll get my lunch."

Outside, we went to the other side of the shed where he pointed, "That's my garden patch and it runs across there to the fence, but I haven't planted anything for the past two years. Been too busy." "Is it that, or are you facing up to age?"

"Both," he replied.

"That's a big garden for one man."

"Well, I gave my produce to my sister and my visitors. Then I always raised enough peanuts for several years so I wouldn't run out in case I was away during planting season. At one time I grew twenty-seven different vegetables. Add to that the wild nuts and fruits, mushrooms, and poke salad and such, and I had more than fifty edible foods.

"There are four acres of cleared land at the south end along the power line. Never used it but a few times; didn't need it. Sometimes my neighbors used it. Several asked years ago to grow tobacco there and were willing to pay a good price. Never let them use it for tobacco; don't believe in contaminating the body with the filthy stuff."

From there we returned to the cabin, going in the back way onto the porch. He paused and indicated the bed on the far side. "Sleep there the year round except in blowing rain and the coldest nights. Two Carolina wrens persisted in roosting over my bed. It would have helped if they had had better toilet habits."

We entered the kitchen, which had been the original cabin. A frame bunk was in one corner, a wood stove by the back door, and a table stood beneath the east window. A cabinet, shelves and a few boxes, and a stack of pots and pans made up the furniture and fixtures. A denim jacket and an overcoat hung on nails behind the door.

A second room, the living area, had been added in 1930 to accommodate his wife. Against the west wall was a double bed, on which were piled small stacks of books, magazines, and newspapers.

"I like a natural state of disarrangement and muss in a home. In a house distressingly spick and span, I have the urge to throw a few books about and turn over some furniture. Say! Have you noticed that many of the new homes have few or no books? Such houses are plumb naked."

By the north window is a small wood stove with the metal stovepipe running through the wall.

"Bought that stove in Maryville for $7.50 in 1920, and it's good as new. It was made down here in Cleveland. The prettiest music you ever heard comes out of it when she's a burning chestnut."

A desk-bookcase is against the north wall and between this and the stove is his chair, a rocker. It had been recovered in green plastic, now punctured and torn from long use. "I bought my chair secondhand in Chicago for $10.00 in 1923. My good doctors, Ted Flickinger and Bob Mynatt have given me a fine replacement. Course, it might be a bit out of place when it arrives, new amidst the ancient." Beside the desk is a trunk stacked with books.

A small rough homemade stand is beside the chair. On it are a number of books including *The Rubaiyat of Omar Khayyam, The Bible, The Constitution of the United States*, Eric Hoffer's *The Ordeal of Change*, a dictionary, *The Dead Sea Scrolls*, and *The Dialogues of Alfred North Whitehead*.

"Omar has been there almost fifty years and has traveled with me. I used to quote him after going to bed in New York until I memorized the whole of it. There are several editions by Fitzgerald, you know, each with a different number of quatrains and minor changes."

"Give me a favorite passage," I asked.

"There are many favorites, one is

> *I sent my Soul through the Invisible,*
> *Some letter of the Afterlife to spell:*
> *And by and by my soul return'd to me,*
>
> *And answer'd 'I Myself am Heav'n and Hell'*

"The Asians wonder why we are so fond of Omar, saying they have far better poets than he. I guess the answer is that Fitzgerald did a fine job of putting Khayyam in readable form. Few others have been made readily and attractively available to the general public." An old kerosene lamp was on the desk, and I asked him to turn on the lights so we could see his books which covered the east half of the walls in shelves and cases.

"Say, did I tell you about the fellow at Sterchi's in Maryville who almost sold me an idiot box soon after TV became available here? I saw the sets in the window and went inside to look 'em over. This young salesman thought he had a ripe prospect and gave me the hard sell and told me he could deliver and install that very afternoon."

"You think it'll work at my place?" I asked.

Salesman, "I guarantee it."

"Well now," I said, "the only electricity I get at my place is from rubbing a cat's back, and I'm all out of cat."

On the west wall hangs an American flag. Referring to the flag, he said, "We're both out of date, that has only forty-eight stars."

In one of the bookcases I counted twenty volumes on Thoreau. Two sets of encyclopedias were there, the 1924 edition of the *New International Encyclopedia* and the 14th edition, 1929, of the *Britannica.*

"They're a bit out of date too, but not as much as you would think," he said. "They contain the work of some fine scholars."

"Do you read much in encyclopedias?" I asked.

"Not as much as I once did when I would spend days with them reading, especially in religion and philosophy. Encyclopedias are deep mines of knowledge, too little used."

A worn piece of plywood, twelve by twenty inches, was in the chair. I picked it up.

"That's my writing board. I've been trying to cut down on my correspondence. Some folks have persisted when I told them to stop writing. I just return their letters unopened with 'Deceased' marked on the outside.

"Say, my belly is rubbing my backbone. I'll ask you to lunch since I see you brought your own."

He got a grapefruit and some crackers from the kitchen. We ate in the front of the cabin where he sat on an eighteen inch section of an ancient upturned log. In front of him was a similar log on which was a flat rock with a concave depression. He cracked his walnuts on the rock and used his pocket knife to extract the kernels.

"Folks stuff their bodies and starve their souls. Have you noticed that you don't see many skinny people these days? I say starve your body and feed your soul. A heavy stomach leads to a heavy mind. Use all your energy digesting your food, and you don't have the get up and go for important things."

"How long have you used this rock for cracking walnuts?" I asked, thinking the depression might have come from his long use.

"Well now, I don't rightly know, maybe forty years. I used to forage along the Little Tennessee River and find Indian artifacts. This is one of them. That hole was there when I found it. Figured I could put it to use.

At one time I had a prize collection of arrowheads, spear points, 'tommy-hawks,' and various stone hand tools gathered over the years. They were on display at Montvale Hotel when it burned in 1933. The day after the fire I came off yonder mountains after a week of camping on Hazel Creek near High Rocks. I poked through the ashes but never found a trace.

"Many a time after a week in the Smokies, walking and living off the land, I would come out tired and hungry. The Pflanzes at Montvale would give me a good meal and bed and wouldn't charge a thing. So they were welcome to my artifacts, but I hated to lose them in the fire. There are a few odds and ends in the house; however, I never returned to hunting for Indian relics."

He had finished the last walnut and his crackers and was peeling the grapefruit, when I asked, "What are your favorite foods?"

"I'm like a child; I can't pass wild fruit without browsing. In the pines there are muscadines which come in the middle of September and stay until October. The persimmons ripen soon after and stick around sometimes till January. Earlier there are blackberries, raspberries, and a few mulberries. I never miss the huckleberries in the summer on Chilhowee. I'm fond of walnuts and gather them like a squirrel, and I love peanuts. These nuts were stored three years ago when I had a bumper crop, and they're still good. Never been much of a meat eater, but I have trapped and given away or eaten a few rabbits over the years. They were rough on my garden.

"Then I like grain, wheat, corn, and soybeans are a favorite, and inexpensive. In the old days I ate chestnuts, especially in the mountains while walking and camping. It was a sorry day when the chestnut blight did its dirty work.

"Course, the garden furnished vegetables galore, which I ate raw, cooked, and canned. I like my food straight from the land. Don't go for this processed stuff."

"Mr. Craig at the little grocery on Niles Ferry Road told me recently of an experience with you," I said. "He reported that you had bought a few items including a loaf of bread and were placing the food in your knapsack as two women waited in line. He said their eyes popped when you squeezed the loaf between your hands into a small package to place in the satchel. As they gasped, you said, 'Just letting the air out.'"

"Well, they puff their bread full of air, and it takes too much space. I've been relying too much on the stores recently. Getting dependent in my old age."

"Do you remember your lowest monthly expense here?"

"Well, before World War II, I could and did live easily on ten cents a day. It costs much more now since I don't have a garden. The least I spent in one month was around November 1940. It was fifteen cents, and that was for soap and matches. I would have trouble getting by on thirty dollars a month now. Yes sir, it's a sight in this world the cost of things."

"I gather that you don't waste much," I commented.

"Don't reckon you could call me a spendthrift. I never spent a penny for tobacco or hard drink and probably not over a dollar for soft drinks. That junk is not only expensive but harmful; it's a pure waste. Thrift is no longer a virtue. I wonder if it will ever be regained. Ole Ben Franklin must be squirming in his grave."

It had been my observation that he practiced economy in all things except leisure, and I asked what practices of thrift he thought all could manage.

He answered, "All waste time, money, and energy chasing after things which often are of no essential value. Folks see the products advertised; the neighbors have them; so they want them. To keep up with the Joneses is a hollow ambition. Who are the Joneses to dictate our desires? The only sound reason for purchasing something is that it is essential for the person, the job, or the family.

"Now, before you ask me to define essential, I'll tell you. It has to promote the basic well being of the family or the individual. What is essential for me is a far cry from what is important for most, and I am not selling my brand of life. But if the question 'Is this necessary?' were raised before every purchase it would curb waste. If this became a habit, it would be a blessing for man and nature.

"Stop accumulating things and there'll be more time for leisure."

"How do you use your leisure?" I inquired.

"I use it in a thousand ways. I'm never bored except when I have dull company. Dull company takes forever to leave. Good company parts too soon. My pleasure is so constant that I've often thought that if I never left these woods there would be enjoyment enough. The pageant of nature is ever in progress here. Say, I didn't mean to run on so."

"Continue running on," I encouraged. "You were talking of how you spend your leisure."

"After sunset I sometimes sit here and observe mother skunk and her five little ones come from under the cabin and move off in a line into the woods. They come out at whippoorwill's dusk and come in a whippoorwill's dawn and have never given me a moment's bother. However, visitors sometimes are shaken if they learn my striped friends are under the floor.

Then my cabin is full of friends. I have time to visit with Thoreau, Whitman, Emerson, Spinoza, Jefferson, Lincoln, Shakespeare, Plato, Aristotle, Thucydides, Herodotus, and hundreds of others. You know you can shut a book when you please, but you can't do that with people."

"Do people need more leisure?" I asked.

"Don't know that they need more leisure, but they can put their time to better use."

"You are an accomplished conversationalist," I remarked, "and conversation is a dying art. What about some pointers?"

"Well, the way to talk is like your company is talking—iffen you kin. Folks like to expound on their pet subjects, and I just draw them out. I've learned much in this way, and I've wasted many hours also. Some of my visitors have nickel and dime interests."

"But you've given them pleasure," I added.

"I wouldn't say that, but it doesn't take much to entertain some people. Now you and I talk of everything under the sun and sometimes we don't talk at all. Conversation isn't always necessary in a ripe friendship. Come to think of it, I've never talked as freely as I do with you."

"It could be," I said, "due to age having worn the lining from the brakes of your brain and tongue, leaving me the beneficiary."

"Both have gotten too loose, for certain."

"You remember the recent visit of Don Whitehead, Pulitzer Prize winner and columnist, and Saul Pett of the Associated Press?"

"Yeh, that was good talk, I enjoyed it."

"As we were walking out, Saul Pett remarked that he had come to interview you and that you had done most of the interviewing. He expressed his enjoyment in the exchange."

"Well, we didn't solve many of the world's problems, but we hammered at a few."

"In your view, what is the most serious problem facing man?"

"Whoa," he replied, "we could talk all week on that one, and we have many a time. Most of our problems are transitory, they flare for a time and are corrected, or the steam is released. They pass. Students and minorities riot, wars come, and all sorts of foreign and domestic crises arise and pass with time. One of my greatest concerns and the most profound problem is that of preserving the earth to sustain man indefinitely. This is a continuing question which is gaining momentum. It is building to the point that action will be forced on us, as we seldom act in major events without crisis. It has long been clear that population must be curbed and that the resources of the earth are limited. Yet we continue unchecked in our bountiful consumption. This is not a temporary matter and not as evident as the Vietnam War, inflation, or civil commotion, but it is a permanent problem which won't go away by ignoring it.

"That question involves many problems, but it must be faced. How soon it will hit hard, I don't know, but it will be with us on an escalating scale for as long as we remain on this planet.

"All our problems compared to this are insignificant."

Realizing that my time was nearly up, I switched him back to Paradise by asking, "When did you conceive of your home here?"

"Well, this land was purchased by mother's father in 1871. I came here often with my mother as a child to walk and pick berries. At Huntington Beach in

California in 1912 I had visions of a cabin here, but never dreamed of such freedom and happiness as it has given me. For forty-eighty years, I have had the feeling that for every day spent away from my woods, I have missed a day of life. Away from this place for long and I grow sick in my heart."

I said, "It's quaint, secluded, rustic, but it would not be celestial for most. The journey in rubs off some of the marks of civilization and begins to purify the body and mind."

"Happiness is primarily a state of mind," he replied, "but the environment can't be dismissed. Without basic necessities and without amenable neighbors and friends, happiness would be more elusive. All I need is here. Enough is a-plenty. No, this would not serve for the mass of men, but it is my Paradise."

As I expressed my enjoyment in the visit and started to leave, he said, "Come again when you can stay a spell."

This was the Paradise of Ole Bert, a welcome anomaly in today's currency of life.

BACKGROUND AND YOUTH

A man develops from a mixture of interacting forces of environment, inheritance, and experience. Although none of these factors yields to precise measurement, all are revealing in a search for understanding of any man. This section sketches the people and the community of Blount County and Maryville, Tennessee, at the turn of the century.

Like most of the south, the setting was rural; life was tied to the land. The crop land ranged from the fertile river bottoms of the Tennessee and Little Rivers to the hollows along the streams in the mountains, with the majority of the people farming the rolling hills between these extremes.

Plowing, planting, hoeing, harvesting, repairing tools and implements, fences and buildings, took its toil in time and labor. In the Spring the cattle were driven across Chilhowee Mountain and up onto the high mountain meadows of the Smokies for summer pasture, leaving the home fields free for crops and hay.

Wild game gave variety to the table in the fall and winter—rabbit, squirrel, quail, groundhog, and opossum. In the mountains grouse, turkey, deer and bear had been hunted until they were scarce. When kills were short or nil, the hunters often filled their game sacks with chestnuts or herbs to sell or trade.

19

These commodities provided seasonal income for many families.

Food was usually plentiful, while money was hard to come by and held dearly. Trading and sharing were more the medium of exchange than coin. Home produce was often bartered at the store for coffee, sugar, salt, pepper and cloth. Labor was exchanged with neighbors in planting and harvesting.

The practice of "make do" was deeply ingrained in the people, to use what was available to perform the tasks at hand. The knife, the ax, the saw, and the adz shaped wood for houses, furniture, barns, fences and most farm implements. When needed items were too costly or unavailable, they substituted, improvised, made do with what they had or did without. It had been this way from the days of earliest settlement in the late eighteenth century and it continued well into the twentieth when the coming of the Aluminum Company of America and the Tennessee Valley Authority altered the life style.

Although of mixed heritage, the people of the lower Appalachian region were principally of Scotch-Irish ancestry. These extremely self-sufficient people possessed a strong pride in themselves, their families, and their possessions. One man was as good as another. They were hardworking, frugal, and conservative. They were self-contained, self-reliant, and self-confident. Honesty was a virtue. Cheat or cross one, and it was never forgotten and seldom forgiven.

In politics they were Republicans, having sided with the Union with a margin of four to one when the

question of secession reached a vote. There had been a
few large farms and a very few slaves. East Tennessee
remained a pocket of Republicanism in the Democratic
South.

They were a religious people, churchgoing, more
religious than devout. They had a deep faith in God,
but lived by Ben Franklin's axiom, "God helps those
who help themselves." When crops failed or good
harvests brought meager returns, when children
sickened and died, when hopes crumbled to dust
under the crushing feet of disaster, there was comfort
in their friends and neighbors who gave assistance and
solace and suffered similar hardships. They voiced in
adversity and sorrow, "We don't know the why of it,
but it's God's will to bring this on us, and we must
accept it." They accepted pain and heartbreak as a
part of their lot, brightened now and then by joy and
laughter.

They found pleasure in the warmth and promise of
Spring, in growing crops and children and in visiting
with neighbors. Talking and visiting was the major
entertainment, at home, at church, and at school.

There was little employment other than farming.
Public work meant working for the other fellow, and
such jobs were few and far between. In 1901 job
opportunities increased when the Little River Lumber
Company located in Townsend and began harvesting
the trees from the northwestern slopes of the
mountains. At about the same time the Schlosser
Leather Company built a tannery in Walland. Labor
was cheap and the days were long. There was a
surplus of willing workers. The tannery provided some

income for mountain farmers who stripped oaks and chestnuts for tan bark.

Their most abundant product was children, some of whom at maturity went west to the harvest fields of Oklahoma and Kansas, or to seek their fortunes in California, Oregon, or Washington. The land couldn't support the full yield of ripened manhood. Of Bert's two brothers, Ned, (Henry Edward) went to Oklahoma in 1900 to work in the grain fields. There he married, later settling in Clearwater, Kansas, becoming a successful merchant and a member of the legislature. Robert went to Indiana and returned after an injury in a logging accident. He became a train engineer for the Little River Lumber Company and later with ALCOA. Bert too went west.

A young woman had substantially less freedom. She might teach, clerk, or serve as a domestic. Her goal was marriage, but this was often out of reach with many young men leaving the area. Usually, however, she found her place giving needed support to her mother or another member of the family, in caring for the young members of the brood, and in household and farm chores. The physical drain on the wife was often harsh and debilitating, with childbearing, cooking, sewing, canning, helping in the fields, caring for the vegetable garden, chickens, hogs, and milking. Her work was, indeed, never done. Men often outlived their wives, who literally worked themselves to death or to the point where they had little resistance to disease.

The widower frequently remarried and started a second family. Bert's father outlived two wives and was survived by less than a year by his third wife, who was substantially younger.

Life was not easy, but with a bit of luck, hard work, and good management the people looked for the year to be a good one. If it turned out badly, they put their hope in the next season. Faith in the future was a powerful influence... the American dream of a prosperous tomorrow. When parents were broken by repeated defeat, the confidence lived on in their children.

Love of country was instilled in each child. "We hold these truths to be self-evident... life, liberty and the pursuit of happiness," "Malice toward none, charity for all," and "Give me liberty or give me death" were among familiar patriotic phrases taught by schools and parents. It was a time of pride in a maturing nation, "the noblest experiment in the history of man." There was a place in the sun for everyone who had the capacity to find it.

Maryville was a busy little town with its dusty, or muddy, Main Street centered on a long ridge with frame and brick stores and houses interlaced on each side. Pistol Creek, like a great hairpin, stretched along both sides of this spur of land, furnishing water for the woolen mill and button factory.

The square brick courthouse sat in the center of town on the corner of Main and Cusick Streets, on the present site of the Bank of Maryville [now First Tennessee]. It was an active corner, especially on a Saturday or when court was in session. Farmers came to town to buy, sell, or trade. Without pressing business, they came for the companionship. It was a welcome break from the routine, a time of recreation, exchanging news and views and talking crops and weather.

Although in the distant folds of the mountains some of the natives lived in virtual isolation, little changed in their mode of existence for a hundred years, the main region was in touch with the world. Railroads and the Tennessee River gave access to markets. A long established weekly newspaper printed the news, and telephones were in use by the turn of the century.

Outsiders came regularly to vacation and drink mineral water at several small hotels in the near mountains. The most popular watering place, Montvale Springs, had its first log building in 1832. Prospectors came and took options on mineral rights in the mountains, but their visions of riches in ore came to naught.

Education was within reach of most youngsters in public one-room schools, several private schools, and Maryville College. Most schools in outlying areas had terms of short duration, often closing when severe winter weather arrived.

The youthful nation was maturing, involved in world politics and economics, becoming urban and industrial, beginning great alterations in technology and social institutions, breaking from the past and forging a different future. Blount County was on the outskirts of these changes which would later shape her and her people. These changes had little impact on the molding process of Bert.

Parents

A wide range of fruits often spring from a single branch of the family tree, and the singular Bert was not standard issue.

Both parents came to Blount County after reaching maturity in other areas, his father in Ohio and his mother in Wisconsin. On the paternal side of the family, John Fushee Garner had arrived in Blount County in 1796 as an early settler, establishing his home near the mouth of the Ellejoy Creek. One of his sons, James, moved in 1811 to Ohio. Bert sprang from this branch of the Garner clan.

Jeptha D. Garner, Bert's father, was born on an Ohio farm in 1831 and taught school for a number of years before graduating from the Ohio Medical School in Cincinnati in 1866. After the death of his first wife, he married again in 1870 and came south to Blount County, Tennessee, in 1871 because of the poor health of his second wife, who died later that year. In 1875 he married Ella Moore and from this union came his second family of four children, of which Bert was the third child.

Dr. Garner was an unusually selfless man, dedicated to the service of others. During the Civil War he served in the military hospital in Cincinnati. On coming to Blount County he sought and received the backing of the Friends Church of Philadelphia and Indiana to establish mission schools in the mountains. His main endeavor in Tennessee was in education. With the help of the Friends and other contributors, he started eight schools by 1878, including one at Tallassee whose teacher was Ella Moore.

For a time during this period he also was overseer of the Maryville Normal and Preparatory School which trained teachers for mountain schools. He acted briefly under contract with the Department of Interior as agent in charge of all Cherokee Indian schools in Tennessee, North Carolina, and Georgia. The consideration was three hundred dollars a year, much of which was expended in purchasing books, slates, and pencils for the Indian children who had very little.

His medical service was administered primarily to the people who lived along Chilhowee Mountain, Christy Hill and Happy Valley. Often fees were paid in goods. His last account book shows payments in corn, potatoes, chickens, eggs, and labor. On many occasions he obligated himself beyond medical aid. After delivering a baby and learning that the family had no cow, he sometimes signed a promissory note with which the cow was purchased, later having to make good when its holder failed to collect.

In talking with a friend, Lewis Whitehead, Bert recounted an experience with Buckshanks Whitehead, one of the large Whitehead family in Happy Valley. Buckshanks worked at Montvale Hotel, walking back and forth across Chilhowee Mountain. "When Buckshanks learned I was Doc Garner's son, he said that father had treated him for flux, or chronic diarrhea, and that thereafter he swore and vowed, far and wide, that Doc's medicine made him heave and puke his insides out, including boot heels and harness straps eaten during the siege of Vicksburg." Dr. Garner was greatly concerned with the wide gap between the rich and the poor. The depth of his feeling comes through, as does his religious nature, in a

paper presented to the Maryville Reading Circle on
January 6, 1873. It was titled "Robbery of Labor in
High Places." The content is similar to Henry George's
Progress and Poverty which appeared seven years later
and was a major influence in labor's fight for a larger
slice of the economic pie.

The following excerpts show strong views, and the
paper embodies the Christian ethic, "Love thy neighbor
as thyself," reflected in his life.

> *"There are millions today suffering for want of
> bread desiring to work while God's vast exposure
> of earth is begging for hands to cultivate, but the
> usurper's title is upon it and it cannot be touched
> without a price, and the price is beyond their
> reach. Then the poor must suffer on.*
>
> *"Labor is man's title to the earth, his title to
> wealth and health and happiness. Down with all
> aristocracies but the aristocracy of labor.*
>
> *"The evils of our false system of political economy
> is so interwoven in our whole social and political
> fabric that it is impossible for us to entirely
> absolve ourselves from it as it overshadows us all
> so that if we should try to adopt a strict rule of
> justice between man and man we would starve
> under present laws." His answer to this great
> and continuing problem was, "But let us correct
> the evil as fast as we can. Cry aloud and spare
> not. In free America the people are the lawmaking
> power. Then let us enlighten the people. Educate
> them up to a just political economy. Proclaim the
> higher law of truth and justice. Raise the*

*standard of moral justice and virtue by
intermixing the precepts of a true Christianity
with the education of the rising generation."*

The doctor was dedicated to education and to giving
service to the poor. It was usual for him at Christmas
time to fill a wagon with clothes and food gathered
from his farm and from neighbors and drive into a
remote mountain area where the hardships were
severe and distribute the goods to those in greatest
need. He waged his battle against poverty in the
southern Appalachians a hundred years ago. In
pockets the destitution still remains, but the coming of
ALCOA and TVA offset most of the subsistence farming
prevalent in the back country in Dr. Garner's time.

Many years later Bert wrote, "I watched my father's
efforts to help people and concluded that he often hurt
himself without benefiting them. Does relief breed
parasites?"

Mary, the youngest of the union of Dr. Garner and Ella
Moore, remembers her father as so generous to others
that he often deprived his family. She recalled one
occasion when they had attended a church meeting in
winter. "When it ended, a cold rain was falling. The
visiting minister was not adequately dressed for the
weather, and father gave him Bert's new coat."

Bert's mother, Ella Moore, was born in Pennsylvania
and grew up in Wisconsin where she later taught
school. Two years after her family bought the farm on
Needmore Hill in Blount County she joined them and
began teaching for Dr. Garner in the Tallassee mission
school on the Little Tennessee River.

Solomon Moore, her father, was a skilled carpenter and farmer, a moral man but not religious. He built their home in 1872 so soundly that it still stands on Mint Road where it was moved by Bert around 1918 after the Aluminum Company of America purchased for their power line the strip of land on which the dwelling was located.

Both parents were extremely well educated for the period. Dr. Garner's generosity and lack of good management left him a poor man, which required him to work his wife's farm in his later years.

Bert was very close to his mother who instilled in him her love of poetry and literature. She encouraged his reading and discussed with him her correspondence with Mary N. Murfree, whose novels appeared under the pen name of Charles Egbert Craddock. Her books were among the first to depict life in the Cumberland and Smoky Mountains.

Bert's close economy reflected more the character of the people of the area than the generous traits of his father. His father's example of poor management was deeply imprinted on him and influenced his living close to the bone and holding to what he had.

Youth

Herbert Solomon Garner was born December 13, 1885, to Dr. Jeptha D. and Ella Moore Garner on the Moore farm on Needmore Hill. The farm was just north of Carpenter's Community and about six miles southwest of Maryville. The woods in which Bert later lived comprised the northwest corner of the farm.

His sister, Mary Jenkins, reported that Bert was the apple of his mother's eye and that she spoiled him. Grandfather Moore was fond of the youth and contributed to any spoiling, if this was the case.

Except for the period of 1892 to 1896, when the family lived on a small farm in the Woodpecker Knobs near Christy Hill, Bert grew up on the Moore farm, which passed to his mother upon the death of her parents.

He attended grammar school at Christy Hill and Carpenters. An excellent student, he was usually the first chosen and the last standing in spelling bees. This educational tool was well used and was a popular social occasion where parents gathered to visit and watch their children perform.

The Garners were Quakers and members of the Friends Church in Friendsville. The distance and roads were such that the journey was difficult, especially in inclement weather. More often they attended nearby Carpenter's Methodist Church.

Bert later wrote that his childhood experiences of sitting through long sermons, designed for adults, was extremely unpleasant and boring. Sunday Schools were still in the future. He attended only when he was forced to go, which was too often. When he could he would roam the fields and the woods rather than fidget through the solemn discourses.

His mother often read to him and encouraged his reading. This influence was effective, and he became a tireless reader. Often his attention to a book caused his farm chores to go begging. Reading was primary and farm work secondary.

Disaster struck him by chance in the late summer of
1895 when he lost the sight of his right eye. Older
brothers Ned and Bob were engaged in a missile battle,
using green walnuts as weapons. A walnut caught Bert
squarely in the eye when he happened to pass between
the combatants. The pain was intense and the
medication ineffective. He adjusted slowly to reduced
vision. He wrote in 1955, "The trauma of my eye
blinding it, certainly affected my personality and life."
Bert attended Blount County High School (later
Maryville Polytechnic School) on West Main Street
(Broadway) in Maryville. He did well in his studies
without great effort and was a member of the baseball
and track teams. In track he was active in the high
jump, broad jump and the dashes.

An example of his school work in his last year of
school in 1906-7 is the following portion of a
composition on psychology dated February 2, 1907,
with a grade of 99%:

> *"Advantages gained from the study of
> Psychology"*
>
> *In the great plan of creation man was made
> superior to all other living beings and placed in
> dominion over all the earth.*
>
> *Unlike the lower animals man was endowed with
> a soul and provided with mental faculties in order
> that he might be enabled to accomplish the ends
> for which he was intended.*

It is the observation and study of the conditions and development of these faculties of the mind that forms the subject matter of Psychology.

The study of the human mind is so boundless and when followed out borders so near to the infinite that we are constantly reminded of the Divine origin of all things and that back of everything there is a directing hand.

We pause in our search for the key of the great enigma of creation long enough to ask ourselves the question. Who is man and for what purpose was he placed here? We learn from Psychology that the methods of communication between the worlds of mind and matter are the means by which our minds are developed. Thus the five senses are the sources of all mental phenomena.

Man's natural tendency is to follow the line of thought that offers the least resistance. This accounts for the large number of bad characters and people who never accomplish anything in life.

A person's life will always show to what his mind has been directed.

Those persons who are responsible for the rearing and training of the young should become acquainted with psychological laws and the process of mental action. They should know the kind of stimulus necessary to produce the proper sensation then perception and on through the complicated process of mental action until the result is some good deed or noble work.

A man is not a man in the full sense of the word unless he has developed those higher faculties which are placed at his disposal. The individual in whom these mind powers exist only in a rudimentary state is or should be classed very little above the lower animal.

The brain loses power by disuse just as a muscle does and if not used at all will not develop. Hence the necessity for early development. A person who knows just how the mind acts is able to understand and interpret the individual peculiarities of others and with a knowledge of the laws of attention one has the power to influence others for good or to benefit himself financially or otherwise as is the case with the business or professional man or in society.

The sentence, "A person's life will always show to what his mind has been directed," is significant as one views Bert Garner or anyone.

His journals unfortunately reflect little of his youth, but the following is noteworthy: "One thing for which I greatly respect my father is that he did not try to indoctrinate me in any respect. He allowed me to develop in my own way."

BEARDING THE COCKEYED WORLD
1909 TO 1927

After completing school Bert taught at College Hill at the lower end of Dry Valley near Townsend in a one room school. Eighty students enrolled from age six to seventeen. Fortunately only about half attended regularly, with a number dropping out as the session advanced. The pay was $35.00 a month. He roomed and boarded with a local family for $10.00 a month.

With a sound basic education, a background of wide reading, and an articulate tongue, Bert was well qualified to teach. However, the chore of maintaining discipline, the task of instructing all elementary levels, the number of students, and the confinement was too much for this free spirit. He returned to the farm at the end of the term, planning to travel as soon as his funds were adequate.

After the crops were planted, he hired on to lay track with the Babcock Lumber Company in Tellico Plains. Each earned dollar was saved until he had enough to take him West. Frugal he was at home and on his travels.

There were wanderlust in his veins and rabbits in his feet, and his greatest urge was to travel, to see what was on the other side of the mountain. On October 2,

1909, he took the train west to Seattle. It was the beginning of almost twenty years of roaming the country.

Normally, one would eventually land work or a woman to hold him, but Bert was able to slip such anchors. Working and moving on became a habit.

"I didn't come into this world to buzz around like a bee in a jug and run the risk of getting stuck in molasses."

His sister Mary reported that as a youngster he was often teased by fellow workers for doing more leaning and dreaming on the hoe handle than using the business end. He often said of labor: "I'm not afraid of work; I can lay down beside it and go to sleep and have, many times."

Most of his later characteristics were already evident: his love of books and of conversation, his inquisitiveness and yen to know what life was like beyond the confines of the familiar, his insistence on complete independence and the freedom to go and do as he pleased, sidestepping entanglements which would fence him in. Endowed with self-confidence and self-esteem, he had little concern other than playing it close to the belt, using his earnings only for essentials.

In Seattle he worked for three months in almost constant rain as a stevedore on the docks. On Sundays he went into the high country when the weather permitted, but the season was not conducive to full enjoyment of the rain forests. He moved south by boat to San Francisco, virtually rebuilt after the earthquake and fire of 1905. One of his first side trips was to the redwood forests, described with great enthusiasm by John Muir whom Bert had read with feeling. He worked briefly on the wharves and with DuPont Powder Company, and then turned south to Los Angeles.

The contrast in scenery with his home country was marvelous. Beautiful, broad boulevards in Los Angeles were as level as a board, lined with double rows of palms and pepper trees with long pendant clusters of red berries. On a Sunday afternoon the streets were flowing with autos. The wide beaches drew him for swimming, walking, reading, and cogitating. It was fascinating country and would call him back again and again over the years.

His work, as always, was intermittent—delivery by bicycle for a bakery, tending spacious yards, or clerking in a store. He later recalled answering an ad for clerks at a department store. The job was bedlam, a white goods sale, with women clawing, pushing, screaming. After three hours he walked out. "I couldn't believe that pack of animals going after cloth as if it were food and they were starving. Yes, sir, it was sumpin awful." After less than a year in Southern California, he journeyed to Oklahoma and worked in the wheat fields. Next stop was Clearwater, Kansas, where his brother Ned owned The Racket Store, handling general merchandise. Bert bought an interest for his only venture into business.

During this period he exercised daily in distance running, starting at first dawn and continuing an hour or two before going to work. This led a friend to brag to the engineer of the local train that Bert could outrun the freight to the next town, some twenty miles distant. The trainman took him up and pressed a five dollar bet. The event came off with much local interest generated by his acquaintances and with Bert winning the race by fifteen minutes. The freight had a number of time-consuming stops between points.

His stay in Oklahoma and Kansas lasted about two years, when he sold back the business interest and turned again to California. The timing of his departure was caused by a young woman who pushed for marriage. Not wanting his wings clipped, he fled.

From 1912 to 1915, he was in Los Angeles and began working in a nursing home, the Rosena Rest Retreat, serving as a male nurse. Here he learned how to care for the ill, an occupation which he later practiced with skill in looking after the sick in the homes of his neighbors.

He also worked in a nursing home operated by the Seventh Day Adventists, where he became interested in vegetarian foods and the use of the soybean and grain in preparing balanced meals. His later use of the soybean and a mixture of ground grain stemmed from this experience as did his predominately vegetarian diet.

A desire to enter medical school at the University of California caused him to send a letter of regrets to Billy Joe Henry, Principal of Maryville Polytechnical School. Bert's diploma had been withheld on graduation for disciplinary reasons. He had refused to make a public apology to the assembled students for an infraction of the rule against walking on the streets of Maryville in the company of female students. He was one of several boys and girls who were seen together on Main Street. The others apologized; Bert refused, an early example of his independence and refusal to live by the accepted standards of the times.

The medical study continued for about fifteen months, giving him a smattering of medicine as practiced at the time. He observed that the good physician often made mistakes and had a monumental ego which was more evident in his practice than his knowledge of medicine.

Bert was an apt student and always interested in medicine. In Philadelphia in the late forties, Bert's friend, Robert Kolsbun, was photographing small organs of the body for the University of Pennsylvania Medical School. In discussing the photographs he was amazed at Bert's knowledge of the subjects. "His information was often more helpful than what I received from the medical men with whom I was working." In the Fall of 1915, Bert returned home after an absence of six years. Both parents were in failing health, and much of his energy for the next three years was spent in looking after them and the farm.

His mother died in 1918. He worked for a time for ALCOA in first aid. The next year, Will Taylor, district congressman, got him a job with the Library of Congress. Here he was employed as a guard and later as assistant superintendent of the grounds.

While on vacation in March 1920, he built a small shack, twelve feet wide and thirteen feet long, and covered the exterior walls and roof with tarpaper. The lumber came from the Moore farm buildings which were on the right-of-way for the ALCOA power line. The right-of-way ran where the house, barn and buildings stood. This fact resulted in a sizeable payment to Bert, who had inherited the property.

It was this money, banked at interest, which gave him financial independence and financed his travels for a period of years.

The tarpaper shack he called his castle or palace over the next few years.

He left the Library of Congress after about two years and returned to the cabin and put it into a livable condition.

Soon he was in New York City living in Greenwich Village and working for the Immigration Service on Ellis Island. His journal at the time records, "I came to New York to be near this great throbbing burst of humanity, but this three-legged city shall not scar me with its brand." The throbbing was too much for him, and he was soon commuting forty miles to work from a farm in New Jersey.

He wrote in his last days in New York:

Aug. 19th, 1922: Poking about the back alleys and ragged edges of N.Y.'s slums.

20th: Struggling with my own half-formed philosophy of life. I can't afford to burden my immortal soul with the petty vexations of the sordid workaday-world.

30th: Sitting in Times Square in the dazzling white-way of the Roaring Forties thinking what fools these humans

be. Saw the moon shining above the
white lights of N. Y.

Sept. 2nd: Home to my castle after an absence of 5
mo. 4 days. Bright moonlit night.

He absorbed himself in activities which gave him
solace from the New York experience.

Sept. 10-13: Fishing on the Little Tenn. River.

Oct. 10-17: Seven happy days and happy nights in the
Smokies and Unakas (Unicoi Mts.).

22-30: In the Smokies with a party of ten.

Nov. 14-19: In the Unaka Mts. passed the Crowder
place to Jeffries Hell thence by Slick
Rock to Cheoah Dam. Camped in a
cave.

In the spring of 1924, he went to Europe and spent six
months seeing the sights of England, France, Holland,
Germany, and Switzerland. He carried his gear in an
army pack, often camping in the woods or sleeping in
a haystack. Sometimes he spent a few days with a
farm family, working for his keep. His cross-country
travel was not unlike that of present day youths who
travel with pack and sleeping bag.

In Germany, he was deeply shocked by the poverty
and inflation following World War I. He said, "The only
time I ever paid for sex was in Munich, and the pay
was in gifts of food for her family. She was a beauty, in
her early twenties, practicing sparingly the only trade
open to her. We spent two weeks together, visiting

parks, museums and art galleries, and doing what comes naturally. Sometimes I have looked back and wished I had lengthened my stay." He related that on the way home from Europe he had thrown the journal of this period over the stern of the ship, saying he was disappointed with it.

Arriving in the U.S., he headed home and was soon entertaining family and friends with accounts of his experiences abroad. The nomad was home again, but not for long. Soon he would be off to somewhere, anywhere, continuing to weave the fabric of his life.

The years after his teaching experience were years in which he was driven by his insatiable wanderlust. He recorded, "The wondersoul is in me, and I must push my lonely way fedderless and free," and "a wind's in the breast of me. A fire's in my heels." From his 1926 journal, the following is an example of his wanderings: "Dallying in Dixie! My range is from Cuba to Canada."

May 10th: Breakfast in Memphis, dinner in Nashville, supper in Chattanooga.

11th: Breakfast in Chattanooga, dinner in Bristol, supper in Washington D. C. (late) 12:30 A. M.

12th: Philadelphia. Inspected the great plant of Curtis Publishing Co., home of the *Saturday Evening Post, Ladies Home Journal,* and *The Country Gentlemen.*

24th: Camden, N. J. Visited Walt Whitman's Old Home Place.

31st: At opening of the Philadelphia Sesquicentennial Exposition. Grand Spectacle. Heard Hoover speak.

July 5th: Heard Pres. Coolidge in Sesqui Stadium.

Sept. 23rd: Bob (brother) and I attended the Dempsey-Tunney world's heavyweight championship fight at the Sesqui Stadium.

24th to 26th: In New York City with Bob.

29th: Hunting for my hound, horse and dove in Richmond, Danville, Greensboro, Saulsbury, Black Mountains, Asheville. Oct. 2nd: Home to my royal palace.

He reported having attended seven world fairs: St. Louis, 1904; Jamestown, 1907; San Francisco, 1915; San Diego, 1915; London, England, 1924; Philadelphia, 1926; New York 1939. Yet he reveals little of his experiences at the fairs or on other travels other than as reflected in the above comments on the 1926 fair in Philadelphia.

These were years of searching for an understanding of himself and the world in which he lived. He rubbed his chin across the face of the nation. "Out to size up the world," he wrote. He observed man as he worked, as he played, as he lived. He saw the places where they worked; he saw the burdens under which they toiled; he saw the anchors of work and family which bound their lives to a restricted enclosure.

He searched for his place in the sun, for a fulfilling occupation for his energies. What he found was a deep dissatisfaction in the way many men spent the days of their lives.

The more he saw of life the more he came to believe that "Life is a drag to most folks." He affirmed his conclusion that he must live not as others thought he should but as he saw fit to live. His objective in his own words: "I am attempting to reach a state of living as near to absolute freedom as is possible in our time and condition of society, and yet render service to society." And again, "Courage is the act of living one's own beliefs."

Although admired by many during this period, most people didn't know what to make of him. A man should work, marry, settle down. Yet Bert was home a few months and then away. He was here, there, everywhere. What manner of man was this, for he was beyond anything in their experience? It was not an unreasonable question, and it was one he often asked himself: "I'm really living. Aside from that I cannot explain my actions."

Bert was different. He was here today and gone tomorrow. When home he lived in a two by four shack that was something to see but not to live in. He was a shiftless wanderer and there was no understanding why he didn't land somewhere. He was "quaire"!

Bert was aware of these feelings for he heard them from his family, his friends, and by the grapevine. It was a time of coming to terms with such opinions, which were expressed for many years. He resolved the question in his own mind, "Whose life am I living? May

I not live it as I see fit." So he shook off the weight of wagging tongues and followed his own beacon, experiencing the essence of living through daily enrichment of mind and spirit in pastimes which were fruitful to him.

"I'm no loafer. I'm always occupied with the important business of living."

"There is only one career—living ones own life."

These were years of searching for meaning to the questions, "Whither, whence, and why? Trying to straighten out the tangled threads of existence." It was a life long search, and he journeyed through minds through conversation, and through whole libraries of literature seeking answers.

Through years of travel, years of testing a wide range of occupations, years of self searching, years of observing man and his ways, he found no place, no man or woman, no employment which brought him the fulfillment which he found in his home woods and the nearby mountains. His search for a place in the sun was over. He would live his life where so often he had left it, on his home grounds.

He would continue his travels but at a slower pace. He would continue his observations of man and his actions. He would watch the world go by and the days of his life spin off. He would do it in the woods and in the fields and in the mountains of his homeland. They gave him a contentment he had from no place else.

WOMEN AND MARRIAGE

Upon reading about Bert's lifestyle, people from across the country often wrote asking him to divulge his secrets concerning the simple life. One inhabitant of the windy city received this reply from the sage, "First, shoot your wife, and second, get out of Chicago." A paradox arises upon comparing Bert's general attitude toward women and his extensive popularity with them.

Mary Jenkins, his sister, remarked, "For one who hated women, he had more women friends than any man I ever knew. What he said about women and how he acted with them were two entirely different matters. He claimed women worked their men to death striving to buy them useless things: modern houses, beautiful furniture, new cars, pretty clothes, cokes, cosmetics, jewelry, etc. He didn't fool me though; he liked women. He wrote to them all over the country and had many women visitors and friends, including a recent visitor who knew him at *The Saturday Evening Post* more than twenty years ago." Robert Kolsbun, his close friend in Philadelphia, described him as "always the perfect gentleman, always clean and well attired and well versed on many subjects. The ladies adored him and pushed him quite hard, but he seemed able to stay out of reach. I recall many times when we were out in the field with large groups on nature hikes, and the girls would want to know who my friend was and would hang around the ole boy like flies at a honey jar. At university lectures, women would gravitate to him, asking questions and engaging him in conversation. Always polite, he would laugh and talk and charm them, just being himself, but the escape hatch was kept open." At *The Saturday Evening Post*, some secretaries from the editorial departments would spend their breaks talking to him. All of this attention created a bit of jealousy among his coworkers, but they grew accustomed to it.

He had many good friends among the women of the local community. These included Dr. Beulah Kittrell, a physician, and Inez Burns, a teacher and author of *The History of Blount County*. Bert took many trips with Miss Burns in search of information for the history. He enjoyed Bertha Jones and Florence Rule who lived at Jones Bend on the Tennessee River in much the same simple fashion as he, without electricity or any "modern inconveniences." He had gone to school with Bertha and had corresponded with her for 40 years or so. Miss Jones said of Bert, "He's always the same; he never changes." He was a welcome visitor at the homes across the breadth of the community, but much of his socializing occurred when friends would drop in to visit at the cabin.

This conversationalist had a knowledge of flowers, plants, books, and local lore and lineage. His ability to discuss poetry, history, philosophy, and current events made him a stimulating companion.

"I'm a perennial bachelor," Bert said. He was too independent, too footloose, too insistent on living his own way and being his own boss to engage in matrimony. He permitted very few extremely close relationships including his own family.

Mary relates that Bert and a classmate in high school were going together in 1907 and were invited to join another couple in a double wedding ceremony in Walland the Saturday following graduation. These plans fell through however, because Bert didn't show up. Many years later, a schoolmate of Bert's commented to the woman who had been the high school girlfriend that she had thought they had planned to get married. Without any further explanation the woman replied, "I thought so, too." Bert didn't contemplate marriage, but he enjoyed the companionship, the walks, the conversation, and the food. This led women to believe that he had more serious intentions; and when marriage was assumed, he fled.

According to Bert, "Kings, women and 'creepers' grab hold of what is near them. You can have a perfectly friendly relationship with a woman, and the next thing you know, you're married. In fact, the poor man usually doesn't know what's happened until it's too late; he is lost, bumfoozled. For the eligible woman, Leap Year is every day, only she doesn't ask. She leads the victim into a snare, from a position of simple companionship into one of complex bondage. Few are the men who have ever proposed; instead they have merely capitulated. However, some men seem to like marriage!" And here is Bert's observation of another aspect of matrimony. "I have nothing against sex except its cost—marriage. The price is absolutely out of reason. Someday they'll come up with a more economical arrangement for perpetuating the race." A 1928 journal entry states: "I'll let no woman make a monkey out of me." Yet, at the age of 43, on March 1, 1929, he married Mote Petty Nifong, a divorcee with three daughters. Two weeks prior to this, he denied that he had any intention of marrying. He told his brother, Bob, "The grandmother of my wife ain't been born yet." Shortly after obtaining the license, they were married by a Justice of the Peace in Maryville.

Mote was raised in Knoxville. She often visited Bert's community because it was also the home of her family, the Rasors. She and Bert had been casual acquaintances since her childhood.

Bert seldom mentioned his marriage, but occasionally he would explain that he had sold her father some land and wanted to keep it in the family. The perennial bachelor lost his footing and went off the deep end.

A week after the wedding he disappeared, leaving nothing but a note in way of a goodbye to his bride. "I'm gone, don't try to find me." After recovering from the immediate shock of his desertion, Mote inquired of Mary as to his whereabouts, but Mary knew nothing of his abrupt departure. Although she had hoped that the responsibility of a wife and children would cool his blood and his heels and make a family man out of Bert, she was not surprised when it failed to work. The hasty escape was much more in keeping with his nature than was the unexpected marriage.

Bert's journal reveals the depths to which his buoyant spirit sank at this time. Out of thirty-nine journals covering forty-eight years in which he expressed abounding enthusiasm and great zest for life, this is one of only two periods where depression shows through. His wife and marriage are not mentioned specifically at this time. However, knowing that he was married March 1st, 1929, and that he left home shortly after leaves no question as to the cause of the depths of his despondency. In Cincinnati on March 12th, 1929, Bert describes his condition as, "Crazed by the agony of my despair." On the 15th in St. Louis he concludes, "Regret is a useless emotion." Here was a man who enjoyed the unbridled independence of the wind. Hence, it is not surprising that wedlock, after a few days, shattered and temporarily destroyed his happiness.

As he looked at his 12 by 13 foot cabin embracing 150 square feet of living space, and as he thought of the wife and three stepchildren to be housed there, he realized that he had lost his insularity. His unrestrained reality had been consumed by the nuptial flame. His spirits plummeted until he was crazed beyond himself. He panicked and ran, catching the first train to anywhere. Usually as he traveled, he freely entered into conversation with his fellow passengers, but this time he was lost within himself, groping and searching for an answer to his despair.

Journal entries in this year include, "Great Jehoshaphat, the Philistines are upon thee," "M-I-R-A-G-E spells marriage," and "Have been forty kinds of a damn fool, but this is incomprehensible." He arrived in California after three weeks of disconsolate travel and went to work for his nephew in Claremont. With 2,500 miles separating him and the cause of his agony, he began to face up to his plight. He wrote and expressed his apologies for leaving and informed Mote that he was sending money so that she and the children could join him.

Ole Bert: Sage of the Smokies

In March 1930, after almost a year in California, Bert returned home alone to build another room and a porch to the cabin to accommodate them. Mote and the children returned after the school term ended.

Life at the cabin lost its appeal for Mote in a very short time. Bert tried to be the husband and father, roles for which he was unsuited by nature and inclination. He loved the cabin as it had been and not as it was, filled with the accoutrements of a wife and family. He wouldn't let her keep chickens, he wouldn't build a road in. What he provided in the way of food didn't include many items from the grocery. They had their happy moments, but a chasm existed between a woman who expected a life in the twentieth century and a man who insisted on the backwoods of the nineteenth.

Bert often took his family hiking and camping in the Chilhowees of the Smokies. The children enjoyed picking huckleberries, blackberries, and raspberries. Mote would gather azaleas, Indian pinks, and Solomon's seal, which she planted around the cabin. She also planted the hemlock in front, now a beautiful specimen fifty feet in height, and Virginia creeper, which covers the yard and climbs high into the trees.

A large garden produced ample vegetables, and he brought in the fruit of the trees and vines to add taste and variety. Paying jobs were scarce, and his work was usually that of lending a helping hand to neighbors in their fields. The cabin had become too confining, too occupied for this blithe spirit. He often rambled the mountains in solitude.

After two years at the cabin, Mote left with the children to teach in Knox County in 1932. This was a planned move, and Bert was most cooperative. The weight of three years of marriage was lifted. He settled joyfully into his former state of independence.

Their relationship was now excellent and continued so until his death. They were divorced on June 16th, 1941, and following is his journal entry on that day. "Spent the night with Mote. Shook the shackles. Agreed to disagree agreeably." By mutual consent Bert had filed for divorce on the legal ground of desertion. More accurately, the grounds were Bert's absolute incompatibility with the institution of marriage.

He continued to visit her and she him in a ripe friendship. Bert was often extremely harsh on women in his conversation. Hearing him remark over a period of time that they killed their men, I asked him to justify this charge, reminding him that he had a host of women friends and a high esteem for his mother and others of the fair sex.

"Yes, I cuss 'em," he said. "They have an unusual talent for getting what they want, often at devastating cost to their men. It arises from the inborn and developed drive to get a mate, feather the nest, and perpetuate the race. Their tools are a sharp tongue, cunning wit, and sex. Wasn't it Eve who talked Adam into the apple and out of Eden? There is often more truth than fancy in fable."

"And you have returned to Eden?" I said.

"I could have never done it with Eve; that's for certain."

"How do they kill their men?" I repeated.

"The secondary role given women and their basic nature has shaped them into scheming, crafty, devious creatures to obtain their ends. Many tie their men in knots pushing them to supply things beyond their capacities. This tender helpmate is often harder and sharper than her mate. With caustic tongue and craftiness she pushes him too far, over the brink to the point where death is a welcome relief. I've seen it happen again and again. I've seen them make slaves of their men, lashing them with tongue, warping them with deviousness and torturing them with sex or the absence of it, driving them through the most atrocious of hells. They're battered until broken in spirit and in body, leaving nothing but a dry, vacant shell.

"Aristophanes' *Lysistrata* of twenty-four hundred years ago demonstrated the power of sex to bend men to the will of women, but sex is not as devastating as a spiking and censorious tongue."

"Bert, I'm convinced that you're half faker. You tear women to shreds and never mention the other side of the coin."

Bert chuckled, "I won't fall out with you over women, but I agree with Kipling that the female of the species is more deadly than the male:

> *When Nag the basking cobra hears the careless foot of man,*
> *He will sometimes wriggle sideways and avoid it if he can.*
> *But his mate makes no such motion where she camps beside the trail.*

For the female of the species is more deadly than the male.

SNAKE MAN

Victor Whitehead and I were walking near his old home place in Happy Valley in the late fall of the year, and he talked of Bert.

"He made you feel good just to talk to him. I shore miss him. When I was a boy, he used to come by our place over there and visit, coming and going from the high mountains. He wore overalls and carried a walking stick, one out of that stack of sticks on his porch. We always liked seeing him.

"Ya know, he hated to see boys or anyone kill things. Said it was against his grain to kill other creatures.

"I'll tell you about one experience with him not many years ago, up the valley here at an old home site grown up in briars and bramble. It was snaky country, and I don't cotton to snakes in no shape or form. Bert walked right through the bushes and briars, but I walked around. Near the other side I saw a huge snake and picked up a rock to kill it.

"He wanted to know what it was I was doing, and I told him I was going to kill me a snake. He told me to wait a minute.

"He came over, held his hat in his left hand and made slow circular motions over the head of the snake. With his right hand he caught it about midway and picked it up. The snake was straight as a board from his hand to its head and level to the ground, with the tail end wrapped around his arm in a tight grip.

"Now, I don't like small snakes, and that was a huge 'un. 'How you gonna git that snake off your arm?' I asked him.

"He said he thought he could manage it.

"I was scared to death with that forked tongue darting all over the place, and he was completely unconcerned. I wanted that snake down and dead, and there he was having a bit of fun with it and me.

"Bert, what are you going to do with that thing?" I demanded. He then knelt and placed the snake on the ground. As soon as it felt the earth, it uncoiled from his arm and disappeared into the weeds.

"Bert looked at me, 'You grew up around here and should know something about snakes, but I doubt if you know what kind of snake that was.'

"I don't care!" I told him.

"That was a king snake and wouldn't hurt a thing, and you couldn't wait to kill it."

"That's the way he was," said Victor.

"You know, Bert was snake-bit over there on Chilhowee one time. I believe it was in the fifties. (September 24, 1953, according to an article in the *Maryville-Alcoa Daily Times*). He was picking

56

huckleberries, if I 'member right, when this copperhead got him on the leg. He was near the top of the mountain and had to go a good ways to the road at Montvale Springs. Anyhow, he got Ben Holder to drive him in his old pickup to Dr. Crowder's. Ben was getting all the speed he could out of that truck and said Bert patted him on the arm and told him to slow down, that that little snake bite shouldn't kill 'em both.

"Bert told me later that the shot Dr. Crowder gave him was worse than the bite."

H.F. Lamon, Jr., a local insurance agent, entered my office one day as Bert was leaving. I asked H.F. if he knew Bert.

"Not too well," he said, "but he used to visit my father and chew the fat when I was a youngster. One day he was in the house visiting when I came in. I was just standing there looking him over as they talked. As I watched, you can imagine my surprise when a snake poked its black head with its beady glistening eyes from the front of his shirt a few inches above the belt. He had it wrapped around his waist. I was so shook up, he had to leave."

Bert was a law and order man, but his affair with snakes brought him before the Judge in Maryville. He had taken a snake to town and was showing it to a friend on the main street when a passing woman became hysterical. A policeman took him in, and a time was set for trial. He was let off with a warning and an understanding that he would leave his reptile friends at home when he came to town in the future.

Snakes and all creatures were welcome in his woods. Skunks raised their families under his cabin; squirrels denned in his attic; wrens nested on his porch. Sometimes he would give a snake the run of the cabin, and sister Mary said she was always afraid a snake would leer at her when she picked up a pot in the kitchen.

Sometimes in his later years, he kept a snake in a pen to show the children who came to his place. He would take it out and fondle it demonstrating its harmlessness to disspell the fear and aversion so many have of reptiles.

"They have their place as do all creatures, and we should leave them be. They are a part of nature's balance and have as much right here as mister man and have been around a heap longer."

1938 JOURNAL

His journals carry such titles as "Garnerings," "The Scriptures According to Bert Garner," "Jot Down Book," "Personal Anthology," "Ramblings and Ruminations," "Field Notes," "Fragments," and "My Book of Days." The following selections from the 1938 journal reveal something of his interests, his activities, and his reading.

Jan. 3rd: Life is my song. When I am old I shall sit in the sun and wiggle my whiskers and rest my mind.

8th: "To him the Sun was a gleaming golden coin—His to purloin. In yonder room he lies With pennies on his eyes." Lew Sarrett

9th: Bright, cool winter day. Read at home. Saw no one. Have a belief free from fixed and final doctrines. Like Thoreau, I have the most and best company when nobody calls.

10th: Went down to Jake Best's right after dinner; found his house open and no one there. Started to search for him and found him 200 yards from the house, sprawled on a bundle of fodder, dead and stiff, had died there the previous evening as he was toting up feed for his cattle. Went for neighbors and called Ed

Griffiths, coroner. A big crowd
assembled in a few minutes. Jake
had a large funeral next day. Age
76.

23rd: My mother's birthday. Warmish. Up before
day to get in full time studying. We
should seek that creative way of
living which meets and removes
conflicts.
The church bell rang at 9 o'clock—
after the above was written—and I
went to help dig a grave for one of
my best little friends—Tom Kidd—
age 9 yr. 4 mos. Bluebirds singing a
jubilee. Sunny and warm. Over to
Uncle Bob Poland's at sunset—they
being all sick.

Feb. 5th: Served on the jury at the trial of Roy Flynn, age 21, and Mrs. Ora Mae Felte, age 18, for the murder of Policeman Bart Coker (Coker shot Jan. 1st). Flynn was sentenced to the electric chair and Felte 21 yrs. in pen.
Can we live unselfish lives when our livelihood depends on a selfish, acquisitive economic system?

9th: People dread solitude because they haven't come to terms with themselves.

12th: "Most churches are holding men back from intellectual progress in religion." Christian Century
Man has reached a state of painful and dangerous maladjustment to nature.
"The Eden Story arose from man's deep racial memory that he once lived the simple, natural, free life of an animal." Virgil C. Aldrich in Christendom

22nd: "To really live is the rarest thing in the world." Oscar Wilde

Mar. 4th: Heard first dove coo.
"Happiness consists of being with nature, in seeing it and holding converse with it." Leo Tolstoy at 23

13th: "The highest philosophy is the art of living." Epicurus
I long since found that the most

61

worthwhile work for me is that
which pays no money.

21st: First day of Spring and a glorious warm,
sunny one. My feet are restless to
scale the heights.

22nd: First wood thrushes singing. And it came
to pass I spent the night in Fountain
City with Mote. Talked philosophy
with John Neal.
My life must be guided by the truth
as Bert works it out.

27th: Home reading Spinoza. Cloudy and cool.
Dogwoods blooming. "All events are
the mechanical operation of
invariable laws, and not the whim of
an irresponsible autocrat seated in
the stars." Spinoza

30th: "Speak to the earth and it shall teach
thee." Job 12:8 31st: At 4 a.m.
Thurs, an earthquake shock awoke
me from sound sleep; it was felt all
over E. Tennessee—no damage.
April 1st: For the past ten years I
have been doing a lot of nothing,
and these years have been the
busiest, happiest, and most
profitable of my checkered career—
so far.
This crazy, greedy, sin-cursed,
speed-mad world is not driving me.
Heirs of the ages, we go chasing

after bubbles, oblivious to our
heritage.

2nd: The Fall of Man is no myth though the
Eden Story is. He falls daily when he
knows right and doesn't do it.

3rd: I must do my own fishing in the ocean of
truth.

11th: First whippoorwill called at dawn. Five
days earlier than last year. This date
is early enough to plant a garden in
this section. Is not the beauty of
nature a more appropriate shrine for
spiritual worship than the beauty, if
any, of ritual?
Church creeds have little meaning
to one concerned with the eternal
verities.
The major business in my life is that
of being a Friend.

12th: "And I talked with Him on hills
listening to the whippoorwills,
But I missed Him on the road
Where His other children strode."

24th: A pair of cardinals built their nest in a
Spirea bush within 8 ft, of my
kitchen stove. Have 4 eggs. Hatched
3 birds 5:07. Little birds left nest for
good 5:15.

30th: "I will lift up mine eyes unto the
　　　　mountains, from whence cometh my
　　　　help." Psalm 121:1

May 1st: "What the superior man seeks is in himself;
　　　　what the inferior man seeks is in
　　　　others." Confucius

2nd: Take all the sacred scriptures of the world,
　　　　combine them with all known
　　　　scientific knowledge and reduce the
　　　　whole to a common denominator
　　　　and you will have a proper textbook
　　　　to reveal God and his way of living
　　　　for man.

4th: Took off on my annual May 4 pilgrimage to
　　　　Chilhowee mts. Lunch near Monkey
　　　　House place. Saw an eagle at the
　　　　Indian Rock Bluffs. Explored "Flats."
　　　　Confab with John Martin, Walt,
　　　　Harvey and Clayton Whitehead,
　　　　Spent night at Montvale Springs
　　　　with Tucks. Visited Charly Blevens
　　　　who is now under the influence of
　　　　Drs. for cancer (so Drs. call it).

9th: The human body and soul require
　　　　privations for proper development.

12th: The only service for which I have ever felt
　　　　properly paid was that which I freely
　　　　gave.

15th: A pair of Carolina wrens are working hard
　　　　today, Sunday, building a nest in

my stove pipe. Their second nest this year.

24th: Am I to submit meekly to the regimentation and slavery that is foisted upon man to a crazy, machine-age society?

25th: Walked cross country to Aunt Hiss Whiteheads in Maryville to mow her yard—home on Shank's mares also. So cold had to have fire at night.

29th: Home alone reading Spencer's "Education" and "Data of Ethics." Rainy—has been a nice showery May for crops— a downpour yesterday. Have fire for comfort this a.m. as I write this. "The defects of children mirror the defects of their parents." Spencer "Our government, as a whole, is about as good as the general state of human nature permits it to be." Spencer Leisure is as essential to me as air, time to muse and loaf. I am not to be exploited or have my emotions played upon like they were a fiddle.

31st: I found today some Balm of Gilead trees beyond "School House Gap" near Mack Kagleys. Visited old Mack, age 80, and wife, Betty, who live right where they did 45 years ago when I used to go to their house for our mail. They and their father kept the Ellswoth Post Office. They look just like they did then and old Mack is a shrewd philosopher. Has radio and daily paper. Weighs 250. Seldom leaves his farm, and has not for years. Lives right where he was born.

My ancestors have for millions of years lived in forests and mountains; why should I live or work in a stuffy, stinking town?

Who is the infidel—the person who says he doesn't believe and lives it, or the person who says he believes and doesn't live it?

June 2nd: As society changes and evolves, governments have to amend and change their constitutions; can Christianity afford to ignore this law of nature?

It takes courage to unlearn things— to take a drastic mental and moral catharsis.

It isn't what a man has that makes him contented—it's what he doesn't want.

19th: As the area of our enlightenment enlarges, it lengthens the circle of the surrounding darkness.

July 3rd: Mote came last eve and left today. For dinner we had new tomatoes, okra, blackberries, cucumbers, lettuce, cornbread, and roasted soy beans. Katydids now singing—supposed to frost October 1st. (Didn't—first frost was Oct. 25)

7th: "What a deal of cold business doth a man misspend the greater part of his life in!" Ben Johnson

10th: At home mostly alone, reading and writing. Dock Giffin and G.C. Petty called. My old hen redbird is setting on her third nest of eggs this season. She knows me and is tame. Have a fine specimen of hognose snake (Spreadhead) in the house.

14th: Worked hard all day with a bunch of Methodists repairing the Carpenters Church (built 1928). Built a concrete wall under chimney and along North Side. The ladies gave us a picnic dinner. This church celebrates its 100th anniversary Sunday, July 24.

17th: Home alone, except for straggling callers. Having plenty of green corn, tomatoes, okra and cucumbers, also blackberries and beans. A whippoorwill sang tonight; it's about the last of their concert season; last year they quit 7-16.

19th: Took off lighthearted and afoot—and alone—on a most delightful reconnoitering trip to Gregory Bald and N. C. It rained, so I ate my lunch at Montvale Spgs. Leaving there at 1 o'clock hiking leisurely via Rabbit Creek Road and arrived at junction of Abrams and Cove Creeks (13 mi.) at 6 p.m. where I camped. Sleeping comfortably with one blanket.

"As oft as on the ground I've lain
I've died and come to life again."

Leaving junction at 5 a. m. via the dandy new Ekaneetlee Gap Trail, arrived at top of Gregory Bald at 8:30 a.m. A profusion of large huckleberries near summit—foggy, cold and rainy— saw lots of turkeys and a glorious display of fiery azaleas about

Moore Spring and on N. side of Gregory. Left the Bald via old Panther Creek Trail—the reddest, most gorgeous azaleas I ever saw here—till I struck the new Sugar Cove Ridge Trail—ate lunch 11:15 at Laurel Bank—thence to John Oliver place where a rain forced me to camp for night—so home via Cooper Road (14 mi.) arriving at Montvale Springs for dinner at Tucks at 11:30

Thurs., July 21st. Rhododendrons mostly gone. Indian pinks blooming on Gregory Bald, also big red lobelia. Talked with Becky Cable, The mts. and I have secrets no one else can ever share.

23rd: "Ef'n loafin' be's so wrong, huccome all de angels dooes hit all de time right befo' da Lawd ! ? !"   Hambone
"Let him rejoice who has a loaf of bread,
A little nest wherein to lay his head,
Is slave to none, and no man slaves for him,
In truth his lot is wondrous well bestead.
Sooner with half a loaf contented be,
And water from a broken crock like me,
Than lord it over one poor fellowman,
Or to another bow the vassal knee."
Omar Khayyam

Aug. 2nd: Awareness of ignorance is the first fruit of ripened knowledge.

8th: I simply cannot "mold" my theological thinking into any pattern written or preached by other men.

15th: I headed afoot and alone for the Great Smoky Mts. National Park. Seed a bear and treed a whiskey still. Home by the light of the pretty moon, arriving just as a glorious dawn broke. Had a good shower bath at Indian Rock. Explored Flats Creek.

"Life's pleasures slipped away from
him
And went their many ways;
He planned so many tomorrows
That he never had todays."
The Bible is a handy book—you can
make it say anything you want it to.

19th: In living in the woods, I'm not running
from life but towards it.

Sept. 14th: Most of life's finest resources are
essentially simple. Most folks have
lost their way in the jungles of life.

18th: My love of God is no more subject to
dogmas and doctrines and
sacraments and scriptures than is
my love of nature.

24th: Hiking in the hills of home, frivolous and
free from the world's foolishness.
Went via Binfield and Mort
Carpenter's (deceased) Sale. I
bought at auction a wool coat-shirt.
Perfectly warm fall day.
"To him who has a hold on vaster
and more permanent realities, the
hourly vicissitudes of his personal
destiny seem relatively insignificant
things."

Oct. 16th: Old man Cagleseems to have attained some
of that calm and serene wisdom of
life which is the ripest and finest
fruit of human living.

70

21st: Gone with the wind to the Little Mt. A
perfect, cool autumn day with colors
gay; so I am too busy to work. Went
via Christy Hill—lunch at The "Little
Mack" Spring and a snooze with the
song of the wind in the trees for a
lullaby.

23rd: "Desire is but an old white goat
That nibbles down a whim, (bush)
And works so hard to crop a meal
He keeps his body thin." "The
Village Idiot"

25th: First frost here. Temp 36 at sunup, exactly
6 a. m. Strolled away to the
mountain. Lay and listened to the
cathedral pines in School House
Gap, where Father built a
schoolhouse 66 years ago. Lunch at
Iron Spring down creek from Lake
Lanier. To Montvale Spgs. Home via
Charley Blevens, cross country
across knobs to Tom Hollow, thence
to Susie McSpaddens and home.
Gorgeous, cool, clear day—like
liquid amber.

Nov. 1st: Gathered my walnut crop—a short one, and
helped Harrie Ray gather corn—
helped him all day yesterday. Crows
began to congregate today.

2nd: To Maryville Town on business and
pleasure. Another warm, clear

71

perfect day. Held interesting converse with many people including Dr. R. W. Lloyd, Pres. of Maryville College; Dr. E. W. Hall, A. E. Cruze, Supt. of Schools, Lanty Ross; Trustee Jim McCammon, Clyde Emert, Editor of "Times"; Hedge at "Enterprise" office, Edd Rowan, old man Richardson, 100 years old— was a slave—; Fred Edmondson, Muriel Wallace and her daddy, John; Mace Bartlett, Preacher Cagle, and Ben Fuller Esq. Visited Brother Bob and Sister Mary and Aunt Hiss W. Home at sundown.
Old "big" Cruze (Socrates) said today he was ratiocinating lucidly.

4th: "Science finds out ingenious ways to kill
Strong men, and keep alive the weak and ill
That these sickly progeny may breed,
Too poor to tax, too numerous to feed." H. L. Mencken

5th: To Carpenters Schoolhouse to a Republican rally. Young John Crawford orated 7 p.m. Previous to this speaking I heard Pres. Roosevelt on radio at Clarks Store, urging the voters of the nation to continue "New Deal" in office.
Helped Lloyd Quiett hand off

tobacco.

A limpid, warm clear day after the heavy rain last night. Autumn colors at their best now—not quite so brilliant as some years due to two month drought.

6th: Another beautiful Sunday almost wasted by visiting hoi polloi. They came all day long till I got nothing read.

11th: Helped Cal. Carp. dig spuds.
"Through clever and constant application of propaganda, people can be made to see paradise as hell, and also the other way around."
Adolf Hitler in "Mein Kampf" page 376

13th: Today read George Selde's "Freedom of the Press." "Advertising is 85% emotional and 15% rational."

15th: Grand clear cool day. Sat up last night with Tennie Tuck Carpenter. She has cancer.

18th: Went to Maryville. Wrote Aunt Hiss Whitehead's will. Paid my taxes. Had long talk with Edwin S. Cunningham in his home in Maryville. He was formerly for 16 yrs. U.S. Consul General in Shanghai, and he talked long and seriously about present international mess—Japan's war in

China and her alliance with
Germany and Italy and against
Russia. Edd says the U.S. will
eventually have to fight Japan. (It
did.) 20th: Jesus said there was no
marrying in Heaven. Perhaps that's
the reason it's a place of happiness.

24th: Thanksgiving Day. Hiked home early from
Maryville— loon happy in the rain. A
soaking, cold rain that turned to
thick snow before I reached home.
Temp 36. Spent last night with Aunt
Hiss Whitehead where I worked all
day yesterday putting a water
system in her house. Thanksgiving
dinner alone—baked sweet potatoes,
scalded cornbread, butter, fried
potatoes and canned tomatoes. Two
inches of snow on ground and much
melted. Read all p.m., as it snowed,
in Powy's "The Meaning of Culture."

25th: "Nor need we ever be ashamed of a life
hidden from the uproar and clamour
of the world, nor be bullied into
regarding it as selfish. Who knows?
Who can tell? It may well be that
Nature herself—or at least our own
planetary Earth—depends upon
such subtle ecstasies in her
offspring for her own indescribable
self-realization." Powy Compromise
might be called a basic and
fundamental law.

26th: Twenty years ago today Mother died. Out over the landscape in the crisp morning air, temp 25, after grist for my mill. To Bob Poland's where I helped George Poland saw down some large oak trees for wood. Bob Pollard and wife sick.

27th: "True happiness is of a retired nature and an enemy to pomp and poise. It arises in the first place from the enjoyment of one's self and in the next from the friendship and conversation of a few select friends." Addison

Dec. 4th: Almost had to swear today as the rabble pestered me and prevented good reading most all day.

11th: My father's 107th birthday. Attended preaching at Carpenters meeting house.

13th: Up at 4:30 for a full day about my business of Traveling Secretary and Observer for the Live and Learn Society. Spent most of today in Maryville College Library studying Spengler's "The Decline of the West." Ate no lunch. Cool, clear. Kicked large holes in the sky today.

14th: Gathering dried hypopalorum (*cathardic tea from tree bark*) on the hills of Hepsidam today. Asked Mrs.

Dockery how Uncle George was. She
said, "If he ain't better, he is gittin
worser."

18th: My woods are a place of continued
enchantment.

21st: In our present economic setup, society
seems not to need my services—
except as charity.
There are too many human
pleasures which an overbalance of
machinery interferes with.
The common welfare is my business.

25th: Aplomb today with the world—visited a bit
in Limbo with Emerson, Lamb,
Powy, and Whitman, also old Omar
Khayyam.
My Smoky Mountains are wonderful
Elysian Fields of escape from the
sordid world of humbug.

26th: I don't see the use of certain sorts of
people encumbering the earth, but if
Nature doesn't know her business
we are headed for chaos.

27th: Bright and snappy with the peaks of
Smoky glittering with snow in the
sun. To Maryville Town for fuel for
my sacred flame. Paid Clyde Emert
for Times for 2 yrs. and went in
cahoots with him on Christian
Century. Held converse with Clyde
on literature and Russia, and with

the following people on various and
asundry topics. Joe Garner and
Nanette, John Badgett, Gene Webb,
Sam Hall, Dick Kidd and Oscar,
Carter Stout (75), Joe Miller (joker),
Carrie Raulston, Garfield Giffin,
Dave Proffitt, and others. Walked
joyfully home, stopping to visit at
Dillon Maroneys, Guthridges' and
Brickey Jenkins' stores and for a
long visit with John and Mrs.
Wallace in their fine home. Called
on Bob, Jane and George Poland—
all feeble and sick. Also Cal Carp.
now ill. Had a sermon from Sam
Craig at his house today.

29th: Up at 2 a.m. to read and write. The days
are too short and every moment
precious. Took off for the Little Mt.
to hunt my hound—went via Warren
Bests—ate lunch near G.
Crowders—8 destitute at Georges.
Long confab with Charley Blevens
and home via Potters in Tom Holler.
The fundamentals of education are
the teaching of initiative,
discrimination, and the ability to
know happiness. F.I.

30th: Rabbit for dinner. Trying to get my visiting
of the sick caught up. To see Jim
Willis West, 82, who remembers
seeing battles, skirmishes, in the
Civil War and tells vividly of how the
wounded shrieked and groaned. He

went to school to my father 68 yrs.
ago, and father doctored him and
his family. Called on the 3 old
Polands.

31st: Time to invoice. My assets and liabilities
just balance— both 0. So I owe no
one. This old body machine is now,
the past year, and all years, clicking
perfectly with not an ache, pain or
care—and my poor, stupid fellow
beings. I live in Utopia, physically
and mentally, and life secretes
constant joy.
I get more poetry from Walt
Whitman's prose than from his
poetry.

"ALWAYS, I HAVE MY MOUNTAINS"

Bert wrote, "If there are no mountains in Heaven, let me go sommers else. These mountains are stately epics of the Almighty, where I have always found a ready grave for my sorrows." When visitors became too many and conversation and reading became stale, he would head for the hills for a day or a week to bathe his spirit in the sparkling freshness of the upland wonderland. He listened to the pipes of Pan and watched angel shapes rise from the hills to the heavens in the morning mists. His heart overflowed, and he reveled in the solitude of the ancient heights.

He sat alone on the open grassy balds and became timeless and in touch with ages past and ages hence through the unfolding waves of ridges reaching to the horizon. Time was shredded to insignificance and he was there ten thousand years ago and ten thousand years hence. Those rolling ranges hadn't changed, and it was yesterday, today, and forever. Here was the fountain of youth, and he drank deeply, shedding time and filling himself with ecstatic reverie in the marvelous world unfolding there.

On the cool clear nights on these highland meadows, with the grass beneath and a blanket above, he was enamored with the display of a moonless sky splashed with sparkling jewels. Orion, Gemini, Cassiopeia, the

Pleiades, and the broad river of the Milky Way shimmered across the midriff of the inverted bowl of the heavens. Brilliantly clear and seemingly close, the starry canopy reached below to the surrounding horizons. He projected himself into the midst of these far-flung stellar beauties. There time was not in years but limitless, being at one with space. He reached back into eons past and forward into infinity. With expansive heart and mind he embraced the whole of it and forged an indelible imprint of that magnificent spectacle into his being.

On the other nights the mountains hollered with the roaring rush of wind and the ground jarred with the crash of uprooted trees. Lightening streaked the heavens and claps of thunder reverberated and jabbed the earth, rolling it as if in pain. Hail came in torrents, shredding the foliage of the sheltering oak. Draped in a poncho he sat, licking the water from his lips as he absorbed the shocks of the storm and thought of the slow leveling process of the highlands under the relentless power of these multitudinous tempests.

He thought about the coming morning, whether fog, mist, or sun. He would welcome the dawn. A dense fog would shut out all but a small island, closing the world in like a capsule, and the ear would become the eye to see beyond the cloud. A hazy mist would expand this island and focus the eye and ear to a larger span. A clear sun ball would awaken the day with the harmonious colors of morning.

He waited to see what the morning would bring. He spent the night enmeshed in the very belly of forces let loose to scream and roar and tear through the hills in wild rampant intoxicated wrath. The experience left him frightfully diminished and overwhelmed.

A mountain safari can place one's self and one's ambition on a different set of scales. The mountains exerted a strong force on the balance which weighed and shaped him. They served to mold his serenity and acceptance of life. They helped to close him off from the mainstream of man and deep involvement. So free was he that involvement and responsibility were anathema, and he became a man apart, an observer rather than an active participant in the affairs of fellow beings.

Bert's earliest youth was spent in Christy Hill in the woodpecker knobs next to Chilhowee, and Chilhowee Mountain grew in him like a root, holding him firmly all of his years. In his teens and early twenties he hit the higher hills of the Smokies with Gregory Bald being his favorite range. From Gregory he strolled the backbone of the Smokies across the broad expanse of Spence Field, up the rocky steeps of Thunderhead, by Halls cabin onto the pitch of Silers Bald and down the ribbed ridges into Tennessee and North Carolina.

If he wanted companionship, he found it at the herder's cabin on Gregory or Spence Field, or at Halls cabin; and he listened to stories of bear and turkey hunts and the often humorous tales of colorful mountain men. He would spend the night and be gone with the morning, absorbed into the landscape of chestnut, oak, and maple, chasing his hound into the dark and hushed depths of the high forest.

Each journey was different—different with the weather and the season, with the fruits of the forest, with some new experience, with some enticing hollow too steep and secluded to have been homesteaded or logged. The moss was thick and the leaves of centuries had decayed and been overlaid to great depth and fertility. In such a sanctuary, Bert sometimes built a lean-to and remained until he turned homeward. In this solitude he lounged, sealed in and cut off and at home with chestnuts and trout and blueberries as his diet. This affinity for the lonesome areas of the hills remained with him, and only in his old age was he prevented from taking these longer journeys into time and into the towering ranges of the Smokies.

One mountain he experienced constantly formed the backdrop of his home stage, a few miles below his cabin. He traveled there daily through sight. Chilhowee is the northernmost range of the Smokies south of Maryville, running like a fence for thirty-five miles from the Little Tennessee River to the highest point on the east end where it breaks off sharply. This range is cut near the middle by Little River, and through this gorge flows the early morning fog which rises from the moist vegetation and is hemmed in by the wall of the mountain.

The rock of Chilhowee was formed half a billion years ago in the bed of an inland sea, fashioned of compressed, fused sediment eroded from more ancient hills.

Bert wrote of Chilhowee: "The view looking toward Chilhowee from my hill is the grandest scene I ever saw." When he lived in Philadelphia, "I miss old Chilhowee. It's worth $10 a day to live in sight of it." And again, "I never tire of watching the changing moods of my mountain." And again, "I shall not complain much of blindness as long as I see ole Chilhowee. It is the daily bread of my eyes."

It was back and forth across Chilhowee that he walked to get to Gregory and beyond.

Indian Rock, also called Smoke Rock, on the south ledge of the mountain was a favorite bathing and camping site when going to and from the higher hills. An overhanging crag provided a roomy, protected shelter, black from smoke of ancient campfires, having long been used by the Cherokees. Over the western end of this ledge flowed a stream of clear, cold water. Beneath it was space for bathing. Here was shelter and a refreshing bath for the sweat-soaked traveler, offering renewal.

After removing his shoes and the contents of his pockets, he stepped under the cold shower and rubbed soap into his clothes, turning full circle. Next he stripped and proceeded to wash each article, which lay under the falls as a bath mat on which he tramped as the water beat into them. Then he bathed himself vigorously. Stepping from the shower, he wrung out his clothes and laid them over laurel to sun briefly.

Body heat served as a towel, and he donned his damp clothes and continued on his way, with the breeze and sun soon drying his trappings.

From the summit he surveyed the quiet cove of Happy Valley. Bare were the ridges intervening between the valley and Gregory. Soon the colors would be different shades of green as the summer raiment of the forest absorbed the delicate beauty of the creamy white of white oaks, the soft pinks and reds and beiges of other oaks and maples, and the mild yellow of poplars. When the colors were gone from the lowlands, he would capture them again in the highlands as spring flowed upward, so he expanded by three weeks the rapture of that beautiful time of the year.

Some years he was in the mountains almost as much as out, and other years his trips were more infrequent. Following are descriptions of journeys in 1941 up the two highest peaks in the Smokies.

THE NORTH SLOPE OF CLINGMAN'S DOME

On a misty morning in the middle of June, Bert set out from Elkmont up the road to Fish Camp prong. At Fish Camp prong he continued up Little River on the fire road which had replaced the old railway. After five miles of leisurely strolling, he reached the end of the road and followed the railbed back into the interior of the mountain. This was an excursion he had long wanted to take up the north side of the highest crest of the Smokies. Soon he was in rhododendron so thick he threaded through it like a needle, crawling where a passage opened beneath, sliding through when the stems permitted and going over the tops where passage was blocked, bending beneath him the tough growth. Progress was slow, and he angled toward Little River which was now reduced to a rocky creek. His small shoulder satchel and rolled blanket caught again and again, further impeding his passage. Soon he was on the rocks in the stream and found the going easy in comparison to the clawing rhododendron.

He had anticipated that the journey would be rough as a cob, and it exceeded his expectations. Wildlife except for birds was absent. A scarlet tanager winged across the creek opening. On the right a rhododendron displayed its purple and pink blooms in profusion.

The incline became increasingly steeper, and water cascaded over rock shelves in the stream bed. The outing had changed from an easy walk to a creep and a crawl, to a rockhopping climb over the slippery stream bed up the wrinkled crease in the mountain. The stream forked a second time, and Bert took the right fork for the left one drained the Mt. Collins area. Now on the Middle Prong of the three prongs of Little River, he would follow it to its source. Up and up he climbed, stopping now and then to rest when his heart drummed too loudly behind his ears.

It was a slow and lung-bursting struggle up rock ledges over which the water flowed in white cascades. He was a good way up the four-thousand foot climb when a small boulder on a channel precipice rolled under his weight leaving him hanging on his belly in the stream, his legs dangling in the cascade. In vain his knees and feet sought support to push himself forward. He could just reach the long leaf of an extended arm of rhododendron. He worked his fingers along the leaf until they grasped the end of the strong branch and inched forward until he could get his knees over the ledge.

Wet with sweat and the dousing, he sat on a rock and dipped into his lunch. His energy had been sapped and the grade ahead was approaching the vertical. He ate and rested and surveyed the surroundings. A silky mist closed off the view below but left the immediate forest of virgin timber clear. The rhododendron and laurel had thinned. Above was a solid patch of umbrella leaf in bloom. The leaves covered the near mountainside in a light green blanket. When he moved on, he observed that the leaves had been punctured by hail. The broadest fronds were at least twenty inches broad on the strongest stalks he had ever seen for this plant.

After food and rest, he resolved to stop more often to conserve his strength and to enjoy fully the excursion. If he pushed too hard, he would close out the physical pleasure which was the essence of the journey. Slow down and absorb it; you probably won't be this way again, he thought. Up the waterway he continued, occasionally taking to one bank or the other where the slope softened and the growth opened. The water had receded to a trickle, and he began climbing over cubes and triangles of moss and fern-covered rocks. Time and temperature and plants had cracked the top two-foot layer of rock for a sizeable area. Each step was carefully taken for the cracks were covered with slick growth, and what appeared terra firma often was vegetation covering cracks into which a foot and leg might descend.

Water trickled beneath the rocks, and here was the source of this branch of Little River. The stream was no more. He estimated that the summit was at least 600 feet higher. It became so steep that he could bite the ground without bending. He climbed by placing his foot on the upside base of a tree, grabbing a strong sapling and pulling upward. How much farther? He moved diagonally to the left to the ridge which offered open rhododendron for handholds and outthrust rocks for footholds. The forest was open but too steep for good footing.

Tall yellow bead lilies bloomed in profusion. The glossy basal leaves were large and thick; yet some had been punctured by hail. Foam flowers and wood sorrel were everywhere, with the pink-streaked sorrel arising from beneath clover leaves. Delicately beautiful was this flourishing display in which he lay for the moment, resting in an almost vertical position with his feet against the base of a giant fir.

The slope soon eased, and the high ridge came into view. He topped out at the tower about three o'clock. The mountain was still bathed in a thin cloud cover, and he missed the grand sight of the high terrain. After a long rest at the tower, at 6,643 foot elevation, he went west on the Appalachian Trail to Double Springs Gap for the night. From there he followed the backbone of the mountain to Spence Field, hiked down to Cades Cove and across it, and on by Cooper Road to Chilhowee, arriving home three days later.

The distance from Elkmont to the top of Clingmans was approximately nine miles, and from there home another forty-two. He was refreshed and ready to dig again into his reading and to cogitate on the inscrutable until his closest associates—the mountains—beckoned again. The sponge of his soul had been soaked again in the lonesome water of the mountains.

UP MT. CHAPMAN AND MT. GUYOT

L ater in September of the same year, he went with his ex-wife and a large party led by Arthur Stupak of the Park staff, to Ramsey Cascades out of Greenbriar Cove.

After returning with the group to the parking area, he started alone at 2 p.m., up Eagle Rocks Creek for the top of Mount Chapman. Becoming entangled in a laurel thicket, he turned and went across the ridge to Chapman Prong of the Little Pigeon River. Up the boulder strewn stream he moved from rock to rock, making slow headway.

After passing under an ancient forty inch log, he paused and studied this decomposing trunk, covered on top with a thick layer of moss. Tree sprouts five feet high grew from the log. Out of decay comes fresh life.

Ahead was a pool framed by the hydraulic power of pitching water from an eight foot precipice. The pool was ringed with huge grayback boulders placed there by the power of past deluges. "Weak as water" was in sharp contrast to the splashing evidence in these streams of the leverage exerted by wild water. For the moment old aqua was tame and chattered in a soothing cascading lullaby as it pitched into the pool. The setting was conducive to a relaxed fulfillment, but to reach the summit, he must shake the enchantment and climb.

Late in the afternoon, on turning a bend in the stream, Bert was confronted about thirty feet away by a large mother bear with two cubs. They saw him before he could ease back, and the big bruin was bristling at the intrusion. Instinctively, he brought out his pocket knife and opened the four inch blade. He realized that this was no defense against the enraged animal, for she reared and snarled and advanced. He backed away slowly and searched for a weapon in the stream—a large branch or a head size rock. The bear was charging, and he grasped a rock in both hands. In one motion, he flung it up and as far forward as possible into her path. It landed with a splash in front of her and she stopped. He was back peddling and seeking another stone. She came forward a few feet, stopped, and circled in the stream.

Bert continued to back up, picked up another stone, and waited. The bear sniffed and snarled. After a seemingly interminable period, she went up the right side of the ravine where the cubs had vanished. Bert took the opposite bank into the tall spruce. After a quarter mile of climbing, he chose a sheltered hollow to build a fire and rest. There he camped, sleeping under two blankets, with a strip of waterproof canvas beneath. Bedding in the bruin's territory wasn't to his liking but plenty of dry wood kept a continuous blaze during the dark and permitted sleep. The forest canopy closed out the sky, and he slept in a black bowl, lighted in the center by the flame and coals.

He slept late and while breakfasting discovered his knife was missing. After a thorough search, it dawned on him that it must have dropped in the creek as he picked up that first stone.

He angled back to Chapman Prong and continued up the narrow stream, over water falls and bed rock barriers in a steep climb. After the stream petered out, he rustled through rhododendron onto the up ridge, through virgin red spruce and balsam with a carpet of moss beneath. About nine o'clock he topped out to the right of the summit of Mt. Chapman on a still, clear, morning. After stashing his gear at Tricorner shelter, he climbed to the top of Mt. Guyot by way of the rough manway. Lunching there, he marveled at the stamina and dedication of Arnold Guyot who eighty years before had measured the elevation of this peak (6,621 feet), as well as all the high summits of the surrounding mountains when this country was primeval.

Yet this remarkable Swiss had mapped and measured the Smokies, as well as the entire Appalachians from Maine to near Georgia in over thirty-five years of work in addition to teaching and lecturing and writing. It was he who first recognized and publicized the Great Smoky Mountains as "The culminating region of the Appalachian chain."

The views from Mt. Guyot were limited by thick growth of spruce and balsam and heavy ground cover. Bert found an opening and had a panoramic view to the southeast. The undulating outline of lofty mountain after mountain extended to the far horizon.

To the north the elevations descend quickly into the Tennessee Valley, but to the south there appeared no end to their eminence. He thought, if you want to see how beautiful the world is, you must come up on the mountain.

His spirit soared as high as the hills as he walked back to Tricorner. There he picked up his gear and went down the North Carolina side via Hyatt's Ridge. On the ridge he found a cherry tree over five feet in diameter. That night was spent on the bank of Straight Fork at Round Bottom. The next morning he walked to Smokemont and caught a bus back across the mountain and home.

PHILADELPHIA YEARS

In 1942 after fifteen years in his woods, Bert returned to the confinement of regular employment. With the war in full swing, the pinch for manpower reached the point where he felt his services would be in demand. He packed his battered suitcase and went to New Orleans and worked for the Immigration Service as a guard and inspector. After six months he learned from a friend in Philadelphia that there were job openings at the Curtis Publishing Company. His letter to Curtis was promptly and favorably answered, and Bert was soon on his way to the only employment which he stuck with for any period of time.

Why Philadelphia and why Curtis when job openings were begging across the country and when he already had a good job with the Immigration Service with which he had worked in New York and on occasion in New Orleans? Bert had a sense of and love for history, and Philadelphia was the cradle of democracy. Often in his travels he had stopped there, visiting historical sites and roaming the streets and places of interest. The founding fathers had forged there the basic instruments on which the country was founded. Why Curtis? Bert had visited the plant in his ramblings and from it issued the American institution, the *Saturday Evening Post*, a close companion over the years. In his library was *The Americanization of Edward Bok*, purchased at Leary's in Philadelphia in 1920. This once popular book is the story of the dynamic immigrant who became the prime force behind the growth of Curtis.

A week was spent at the cabin and in visiting friends across the countryside. The gray, frame shack where he had spun a strong and comfortable web in which he nestled in harmony with the simple world about him had etched a firm hold on his being. The thread would stretch but never break, always exerting a powerful force.

When it was sold in 1969, Leary's was the oldest used bookstore in the United States. Many books from Bert's collection were labelled "Learies, Phila." below his name. The above photograph was taken in 1910.

He arrived in Philadelphia on May 15th and took a
room on 15th Street across from the old Quaker
Meeting House. No time was wasted in settling into the
routine he would follow. He attended service at the
First Unitarian Church the next morning. The
afternoon was spent at Independence Square at a
Patriotic meeting during which the Liberty Bell was
rung, an infrequent happening. His club, the public
library, captured his evening.

On Tuesday, May 18th he noted, "Began working for
Curtis Publishing Company. They didn't ask me to
write any *Saturday Evening Post* editorials this week.
Best of working conditions in this plant." This is one of
the few references to his job during the more than six-
year tenure at Curtis. Continuing from the journal for
Saturday, May 22nd, "To the zoo to see relatives;
thence hiked about Fairmont Park and spent most of
PM in art museum." The work was routine, packaging
and unpackaging, crating and uncrating incoming and
outgoing manuscripts, printing, and paintings. Here
he met Norman Rockwell and received and shipped his
paintings, a trademark of the *Post*. The work as a
shipping clerk was routine, and his mind was often
distant from the tasks his hands performed. The days
slipped by with his associates chatting of their female
conquests and mundane affairs while Bert focused on
what he had read the night before, the evening
philosophy class, a pending lecture, or a planned walk.

He had little in common with his fellow workers, but
he became known in the upper offices because of his
plain dress, his quiet dignified manner, his broad
knowledge, and his simple ways. Personnel from the

editorial departments often came down to talk with him during their breaks. They were fascinated by this refreshing personality.

It is difficult to imagine this intellectual being buried for six and a half years in routine physical employment. Yet the work was confined to five days a week, and he shed the confinement to walk the streets, the fields, and the parks in the evening. He exercised his limbs. He stretched his mind in the libraries, in the University of Pennsylvania evening courses in philosophy, religion, and astronomy. He seldom missed a lecture, regardless of subject, given by a major personality. He conversed with all types of people and often gained audience with religious leaders whom he admired. It was a period of work, a period of study, of change, and of growth. He was absorbed in following new threads of philosophy, religion, and science.

His friendship with Robert Kolsbun, head of the department of photography for the *Saturday Evening Post,* became a strong influence and developed into a lasting relationship. The friendship was deep, growing slowly and firmly. They were alike in that they were loners with a wide range of interests. Yet, they were opposites in many respects. Bert was shy and seldom argumentative. Bob was caustic, extremely argumentative, a rabid Democrat as opposed to Bert's Republican view on all issues at that time. Yet these opposites forged a classic friendship which enriched both during that period and continued to the end.

Kolsbun and I met in 1970 when Bert was near death, and we have since carried on a correspondence from which much of the following comes.

He wrote, "I recall the night 'Tennessee' passed on... I had a dream that we were sitting on one of our logs in a chestnut grove deep in conversation, when all of a sudden, unlike his usual self, he got up and started to walk along the path of ferns and flowers. I recall, I wondered about his sudden departure and asked, what was the hurry? Looking straight ahead he said, 'I have a rendezvous with death and I have to be on time.' The next day or so I received a notice that he had passed on. Strange that I should have this dream about the same time as his departure. In a way, however, it was not strange at all, considering our many years of togetherness." In Bob's words, "When I first met Tennessee (Bert), I was in my fiftieth year, spry and full of spunk, physically active and dedicated to the art of illustrative magazine fotography.... My department was located in the basement adjacent to shipping where Tennessee was nailing lids on boxes for shipping paintings to artists and returning manuscripts to writers.

"I recall seeing him the first time while he was packing a painting while five or six of the shipping employees were jabbing in his ear. I am not one for sudden friendships even though I found some gentle and delicate expressions in this long legged fellow who, when he could, kept to himself. One afternoon as I was entering the foto department, this kindly gentleman came over and asked if I would address some envelopes for him on the typewriter. As the days went by when we passed, we would exchange greetings. As the moments of greetings grew longer, we found we had some special interest.... I saw that he was a loner seeking companionship and was wide open for company. We soon realized that we found ourselves sharing the common denominator of a lasting friendship. It wasn't long before the employees of the Post called us Damon and Pythias. When one of us was missing, they asked, 'Where is Damon or where is Pythias?'

"As the early spring turned into warm summer nights, we were out hiking and having our dinners on the bank of some rambling brook. Later on, I Left the *Post* and went to work for an advertising company. The absence from the *Post* made our friendship all the stronger. From the first, our ideas clashed. It seemed that I was ahead of him in ideas, some of which, I confess were outlandish. In our disagreements, he was always friendly, never taking me to task in any unfriendly manner."

Of their friendship Bob wrote, "He was the best friend I ever had, always considerate, always dependable. . . . Regardless of what measure we put on his life, for me his acquaintance was a blessing. During those Philadelphia days, working conditions were not at all perfect and living without him would have been bleak. His companionship and friendliness made life livable. The strange part of our friendship was that we agreed esoterically on most everything, tho we appeared to be thinking and acting in opposite directions. There was that firm conviction that we were one in spirit."

Although Kolsbun and I both knew him well, a quarter century separated our views. Bert was the same, and he was different. Robert saw shades of him which were gone or never revealed or recognized in my acquaintance. Much that I learned about Bert was never mentioned nor observed by Robert. We were aware that neither saw the whole of him. Does anyone reveal or can he show all shades and depths of himself even over a long period of time? Few men are that transparent, and it is the exceptional man who knows himself. We recognized that Bert ran deep and that much about him remained unseen.

Robert never was informed of his marriage or of his journals. He relates, "I was never aware of his journals. He never spoke of them. Many times I tried to push him into writing articles for various magazines, even the *Saturday Evening Post*. The editors were that much interested. I was always made to understand by Bert that too much was being published, and he didn't want to clutter up the world with more." In answer to my request for information about his job at Curtis, Bob answered, "He wanted nothing of importance, no appointments, no management, no leadership. He was satisfied in just making packages for shipment, wrapping and nailing boxes together. He tried to live in the dim lamplight, but his star was bright and lit up the whole basement department. Of all the people, he was THE personality. He had a special charm and a special grace which one seldom sees down the pathway of life. He had nothing; yet he had everything."

Although Robert often exaggerates, he is a keen observer and the word portraits he paints catch the details and are extremely revealing. Bert was seldom bothered by illness, but on failing to show up for work for several days, Bob was concerned. He sought out his room, now on 10th Street, in what Robert described as one of the worst parts of the city.

"He was the kind of a guy who would never tell anyone he was not feeling well. To him it was bad manners to dwell on sickness, something of a disgrace.

"The room was located above a little Jewish store. I didn't know the exact location so I went in the store and asked the kind old Jewish lady if she could tell me where Garner lived. 'Yes, upstairs.' The stairs, heavens above, were like walking on rubber ice, waving up and down with the tune of continuous squeaks. The trip up was dark, like walking thru a tunnel. A stranger, like myself, making the first trip should have had a flashlight, but I played it by feel.

"I wandered about the hall and found a light from under a doorway. I knocked, never believing who I would see... yep, you are right, it was Tennessee. He had just jumped out of bed and looked like the devil himself, no teeth, no shave, no socks, no shoes, no pants, and the room looked a mess.

"The room, not over five by eight was, except for the one light, dark and dingy. Just plain walls, paper coming off in parts, no pictures. There was one window and that opened up to a brick wall of the adjoining building—none of his beloved sunshine... hardly enough air for two microbes. Under the bed, just a cot, were piles of books that he had purchased from the famous book store, Learies in Philadelphia, boxes of books at each end of the bed. The table was covered with more books and I wondered at the time how in the world he could do any reading with such a dim lamp, no more than a thirty watt. I asked him about the light and he said that was the only one the landlady had to spare. (The next day I brought him a sixty watter.) At such a sight, I told him to get the hell out of there and get some better living quarters, but he said that it was all right for the time being as he was going back to his cabin. (He stayed three years more.) In this strange and imperfect world, it is hard to understand how a fellow of Tennessee's caliber could live in such gloom without a moonbeam or a sliver of sunshine.

"In Tennessee, you have a very controversial person. As far as I can recall, he never for one minute lost his personal identity amidst the ludicrous and frightening shadows of today's living. He was a fellow of many characters, many hidden and unexpected to his fellow man and regardless as how he lived his life, no one could help but love him."

Robert was deeply shocked at the closeness and sparseness of Bert's quarters. Yet, this was in keeping with the way he had always lived when working in cities. The thirty watt bulb gave as much or more light than his kerosene lamp at home. The dark hallway brings visions of the pine-enclosed pathway into the cabin and the nights he walked it without illumination. What shocked Bob was no problem to Bert. It was the way he chose to live. One of his primary goals at this time was to put away funds to provide economic security for old age. The last thing he wanted was to be a financial burden on anyone, and routinely three quarters of his earnings went into U. S. Savings Bonds. He often expressed a strong desire to be back in his hills. "Let me go to the Smokies where human problems don't matter. I must go there and get in deep primal harmony with the forests and solitude."

This was his last chance to salt away enough to carry him through his declining years, and he remained with

Curtis Publishing Company until his savings were adequate to see him through.

Home and the mountains were always tugging at his heartstrings. The still, misty beauty of the Smokies was ever vivid in his mind and longings. The rising ridges and rolling hills of home were indelibly printed in his being. It was with great determination that he buried himself in the mass of men and machinery and grating sounds of the city for so long a period. It was the best of times and the worst of times for this individualistic loner. It was the best in the mind stretching opportunities, and worst in the length of confinement of job and city.

He escaped his bounds at every convenience, and the opportunities were numerous. He walked the streets as he did the paths and roads at home and knew every park and plot of public grass and woodland in and adjoining the city. Yet, his thoughts were tied to home:

"Why waste these glorious autumn days buried alive in a dusky 13 story cave? I must escape this horrid city and get my feet on the ground where I can chop wood, dig in the earth, and pitch hay under the sky and clouds. I cannot spare my moonlight and my mountains for the best man I am likely to get in exchange. Like a man in jail, life for me begins when I escape Philadelphia. The best thing about any city is its facilities for getting out. I see my way clearly before me. It leads to my ancestral woods." His moods were not always in this vein, for he treasured the varied experiences which the city offered. Usually he was taking two night courses each week in philosophy, religion, or astronomy. His philosophy began to jell along the lines of humanism. David Arnold, a

philosophy instructor for the University of
Pennsylvania, was a teacher and became a close friend
with whom Bert delighted in talking philosophy,
always a central interest.

He attended churches of all denominations and wrote
on Christmas Day 1943, "Strange irony—no Protestant
Church was open to celebrate Christ's birthday—so I
had my choice of a cathedral or a synagogue and
chose the latter. Attended regular morning worship
(Sat. their Sabbath) at Temple Kenneth Israel on N.
Broadway St. Received more spiritual inspiration and
far more poetic elation than from most Christian
services. Rabbi Klein preached a splendid sermon and
extolled Christ as a great teacher—which he was."

Religion, like philosophy, intrigued him and whatever
city he was in, he would attend various services to
view the preaching and the practices. Philadelphia was
no exception, and following are a few of his many
comments on churchgoing:

10-24-43 "Toddled to church 3 times today. Almost
feel wings sprouting. In A.M. to Germantown Unitarian
Church to hear the great Halford E. Luccock, deliver
one of the best Sermons I ever heard. In P.M. attended
4 O'clock vesper service at Old Christ Church—
Episcopal—established in 1695. A very fine sermon on
the social and economic responsibility of the U.S., in
their torn world. To Big Library to read, thence afoot to
Broad St. to Masters St. Gospel Tabernacle at 7:30 to
hear the pastor bray like a jackass about the faults of
'Jehovah's Witnesses.' He showed more weakness than
they."

10-31-43 "To Germantown to hear Falfrey Perkins preach on 'Where There is no Vision the People Perish.' Very apropos for we have little vision than selfishness."

His favorite services were Unitarian and Quaker, but he visited them all and made a special effort when an outstanding speaker was to appear. Rufus M. Jones, an important leader of the Quaker Church, whose many books Bert had read over the years, he often heard and conversed with. Of him he wrote, "One of my most cherished blessings was the acquaintance of Rufus M. Jones, a grand old Quaker, during his later years in Philadelphia." Although his life was more varied and the stream of ideas more flourishing, he lived as simply as he did at home. Occasionally he ate at a cafeteria or restaurant, but usually he ate lunch on a bench in Washington Square and his evening meal beside the stream in Wissahickon Park.

"Formal dinner in Chinatown with artist Kolsbun, then to his studio at Y for a session of philosophy and pictures."

"Dined sumptuously in my room on soy crackers, apples and ground raw peanuts. These three food items constitute almost a perfect diet."

"With Bob Kolsbun to creek at Chestnut Hill Ave. Ate a gorgeous supper standing under giant poplars foolhappy in a torrent of rain. We soon dried off and had a fine evening. For supper we had olives, peanuts, oranges, tomatoes, a big cantaloupe, box of crackers, and 2 packages of popcorn."

Most of his food—cheese, carrots, crackers, peanuts, and fruit—was purchased at the corner grocery, and eaten when hunger poked at his ribs wherever he might be in his wanderings. When he returned from his annual two week vacation at the cabin, he brought back an ample supply of ground soy beans, wheat and corn, as well as peanuts, and often the meat of black walnuts. This, with crackers, bread and fruit, sustained him for weeks, broken by an occasional cafeteria meal.

His expenses were minimal, running an average of $15 a week. The rest of his income was saved for economic security and independence in old age. He was spic and span, happy, kicking up his heels, giving joy and pleasure wherever he went, absorbing everything about him and living as lean as a hound. He exercised great discipline and thorough master of himself and thus gained liberty in his confinement in Philadelphia. In 1945 he wrote, "For me life has never been so satisfying and worthwhile, not withstanding the horrors of a hellish city like Phila." It wasn't that the city was so hellish as it was that all cities were horrors to Bert after a brief span of time. So it had been with New York, Washington, Seattle, San Francisco, Los Angeles and every city in which he had worked.

His clothes were not the fashion but were selected with care for strength and durability. He seldom purchased more than one item at a time and only after he was satisfied that it was needed and would give long service. In September 1948, he wrote, "Wore my old blue serge coat all day, and it felt good. This coat was tailored in Phila in Sept. 1926." Bert's basic shyness didn't often show through, and it was some time before I was aware of this trait. He would often ask me to stick around when visitors other than old friends were coming. At first I declined, knowing that the callers were interested in him. Later I would remain when possible.

The loss of sight in his right eye was possibly a significant reason for this characteristic. His love of reading and of walking was such that damage to the other eye would have been catastrophic. Kolsbun comments, "I often wondered if the accident of losing his eye did not prey heavy all through his life. Might that be one of the causes for much of his shyness, his non-combativeness, fearing it might come again?"

In the same letter on the same subject, he reveals another side of the man

"Speaking of shyness, he was the number one and yet, when the chips were down and if the moment was right, he could get off something very striking. One time we went to a religious meeting where each week a minister of different denomination would expand his special theory. This one time I think it was a Methodist minister and he was surely wound up, giving the impression that he had a special pipe line to the Old Man. During the question period, the minister was asked some pretty stiff questions, some for information and others to create a bit of levity. For the first time and the only time I knew him, Tennessee got up and asked a question that lead to another and another... it went something like this...

'Why should I go to your church and hear your sermons when you only repeat the same old line that has been repeated over and over again? You say that I should sacrifice my one or two hours once a week— what for? Thoreau wrote, 'I have been astonished to observe how long some audiences can endure to hear a man speak on a subject he knows nothing about, as religion for instance.' Tell me what you know that I do not?' The minister's eyes rolled with glee, thinking the ball was rolling right in his corner and was ready to give Tennessee the full blast, when Tennessee came up with the steam roller saying, 'What do you know about heaven that I do not? What do you know about angels I do not? What do you know about the devil that I do not? What do you know about the hereafter that I do not? What do you know about God that I do not? Are you not acquainted with the primeval seas we all came from?' I never saw Tennessee so wound up and I was getting restless in my chair and wished he would let up on the poor old minister. 'What you know comes from books and kooks with their wild imaginations. You promise something you cannot deliver. Bah!'

"Of course, the audience was delighted and said so in their applause. The minister, poor soul, was sinking deeper and deeper into the quagmire that he himself created. After a few more questions from the audience, the minister gave up, told the crowd that they were a bunch of damn atheists and wanted no more to do with them. He left the hall in disgust, leaving his hat and, from what I understand, never came back for it.

"In the back of Tennessee's mind, there were things lying dormant a long time, because he was either too shy in telling others off, or because he did not wish to hurt the feelings of others." The following reveals something of Kolsbun's astute eye, an essential trait in his profession, through which he viewed the uncommon Bert. It also unveils one of the many shades of his subject. Bob relates, "One evening he came to my room in the YMCA looking somewhat different, very much the inner man he always wanted to hide. I got out the camera and demanded him to sit still and, believe it or not, he turned out to be my best subject, doing just what was instructed. These pictures were the real Tennessee and they turned out to be prize winners, exhibited in many fotographic salons around the country, bringing in blue ribbons. Did you ever see the pictures? They reminded people of the face of Abraham Lincoln during his tragic days during the Civil War, together with a mysterious depth of spirit."

It was through Kolsbun that Bert became interested in and began to broaden his knowledge of mysticism and the religions and philosophies of the East. Robert was fascinated by the esoteric and had long been engaged to eastern thought. Bert's interest had been on the surface with his information secured from the encyclopedia and the summaries from books on religion and philosophy.

After his departure from Philadelphia, he began to read more closely in Zen, Buddhism, Confucius and Laotse. He wrote later, "The secret of Zen lies in accepting the world as it is. I practice it like most people practice Christianity—only making a stab at it.

"He continued reading in and conversing on eastern religion, selecting from this work the gems of thought which rhymed with his.

He never became a practitioner of any body of eastern religion, but he found much which meshed with his own creed. Of Shinto he says, "It offers no set of dogmas, has little creed; it neither threatens hell nor promises paradise." There was much that he admired in the eastern philosophies.

In fact, Bert's own way was not distant from the eastern way for he too lived the inward life, while laughing and poking fun at the foibles of man.

His departure from Curtis was long planned, and he frequently refers to the intervening time remaining. On October 15, 1947, he wrote, "Two years from today, I'll neither toil nor spin." After giving a month's notice, he left Curtis on October 7, 1949. His fellow workers gave him a big party and gifts. The gift of which he was most proud was Bartlett's Familiar Quotations, for his own copy was falling apart.

The following day he left by Greyhound for Washington, getting off at the stop near Oxford where he walked into the grass to wipe the dust and dirt of Philadelphia from his shoes. In Washington he visited the White House, and the Blair House, where the Trumans were staying during the rebuilding of a portion of the presidential home. Then he went to the Jefferson Memorial, to the Smithsonian, the National Gallery of Art, and the Archives Building. It brought memories of his days at the Library of Congress when these buildings, except the Jefferson Memorial, were favorite haunts, especially the Smithsonian and the Gallery of Art.

He met Mote, his ex-wife, and dined with her at a restaurant on Connecticut Avenue. The next day he stopped in Charlottesville and visited Monticello.

He arrived in Maryville at 5 P.M., after detouring through North Carolina. "Home happy across the dry fields to my heaven in the woods. The cabin is in good

shape except for roof and
screens. Sailed into the
harbor with colors flying."

He was home.

COMPLETELY UNGLUED

He was home again in the secluded cabin, closed in by his old forest of virgin timber. The first days were spent getting the cabin in order and visiting friends and neighbors. Occasionally, he helped Hugh and Hubert Young hand off tobacco and pull corn. It took a while for his return to be known, and visitors were few until the word spread.

He walked barefooted through the woods and assessed the storm damage to the trees over recent years. With an ax and a small crosscut saw he began cutting the wind-felled oaks and hickories near the cabin, laying in the winter's wood. Walnuts were gathered and spread to dry in the sun for later hulling. Persimmons were plucked and relished.

Yet, the contentment he had anticipated eluded him. A heaviness settled upon him that he couldn't shake nor identify, a foreboding that was unfamiliar. His spirits fluctuated, but were never high, sinking lower and lower to his abject consternation. He faked good humour with visitors, but his temperament plummeted when alone.

He attended the Fall Banquet of the Smoky Mountain Hiking Club and visited with many old timers with whom he had hiked and worked in clearing the Appalachian Trail in the Smokies in the late twenties.

Harvey and Anne Broome of the hiking club came to call and Bert talked of his walks in the White Mountains and across Mount Katahdin in Maine the year before. Harvey told of his most recent visit out west to Mt. Olympus and the rain forests of the Washington Coast and of the Wilderness Society, of which he was a founder and Vice President, and their efforts to preserve wilderness areas. Friends and neighbors came more frequently. Sister Mary spent time at the cabin, cleaning and cooking.

Several trips were made with members of Carpenters Methodist Church to gather stones at the base of Chilhowee for the new church. Still he couldn't shake the lethargy that sapped his zest for life and left him empty. He was sinking into himself and couldn't break free of deepening despondency.

He began to spend much time at his sister's to escape callers and to wait for a reawakening. The vibrant, enthusiastic and cheerful Bert was gone. The homecoming with its promises and expectations had turned sour in his soul, and he thought of Thomas Wolfe's "you can't go home again." What happened? What was the cause of this agony? The answer is not clear for his journals, while displaying the despair, never mention the cause. The answers came from his friend, Robert Kolsbun, and from his sister. In reply to my questions on the subject, Bob wrote, "One day I found a plain postcard in my box from 'Tennessee,' saying that he had been advised that he had cancer. I saw a distress signal and left for Maryville within the hour after calling my office to tell them where I was going and that I would be back when they saw me.

"I drove all night, nonstop, in low spirits with visions of seeing my friend, a dying man. Never will I forget the moment I arrived the next afternoon in a pouring rain and saw him sitting on sister Mary's porch. He was beaten, chestfallen; he was completely unglued. It was one of the most pitiful sights I ever hoped to see.

"This was not my old friend 'Tennessee'—this was a ghost, not even his ghost. Mary saw my hungered condition and right away put together a delightful meal.

"Afterward, I gave him almighty Hell for letting the quacks get him down to such a deplorable state. Look at you," I said, "you are a disgrace. At 64, you're falling apart. Come out of it and let's go to the cabin and count raindrops." We went, lit a fire in his rickety stove and before long his spirits began to rise, at least there was promise that he might overcome the sad state of despondency."

Bob remained two days. Bert had been surprised to see him. He was not one to make known his health problems. The fact that he wrote Kolsbun discloses the strength of their relationship and the significance of their close companionship in the years just ended.

To send a call for help was against his whole nature and demonstrated how dark was his prostration at the time. Depression was so foreign to his nature that he was devoid of the normal defenses and lost in the clouds of his despair.

Kolsbun also reported that Bert had had a prostate operation in Philadelphia the year before and had mentioned cancer once. His journals make no mention of this nor do they reflect any change in mood in Philadelphia.

His sister remembered this agonizing period and the spectre of cancer, his moping and loss of self. She recalled Kolsbun's visit and that Bert was flabbergasted that he came and saw him in such a wretched state.

It was the dampening vision of a disease which he feared would pluck from him the joy of home and the hills for which he had longed for seven years, the leisure and the enjoyment of living as he liked in harmony and contentment, that was the prime cause of his misery. His dreams of pursuing his desires unrestrictedly were overcast by imagined prospects of being cut short before fulfillment.

Another probable cause was the abrupt shift from one life to another. It took time to adjust to the change in pace from Philadelphia to Needmore Hill, from a schedule of work, lectures, studies, reading in well stocked libraries to the still quiet of his paradise.

The journals disclose that the depression was severe from December, 1949, until early April of the following year. On the 22nd of December he visited his doctor, and his decline begins to show through. On Christmas Eve he wrote, "I walked and walked in my pretty woods and communicated with my trees—very melancholy." On December 30th, "I walked in my woods in bright moonlight. I lived centuries in this night." The next day's entry, "A gorgeous morning, but I'm in mortal agony. The year is about finished and so am I perhaps." This tone continues until the first of April when he wrote,

"Much enrapport today. Out of the valley and on the heights again." His draped spirits slowly unfurled and began to wave briskly in the gentle breeze of contentment. For four long months he waded through the haunting gloom of depression. He was home where he had longed to be, but Paradise turned to Hades until he rode it out.

About twenty years later as we began a walk on a mountain path, Bert told me that he couldn't remember being in the dumps and didn't know what it was to be depressed, a condition with which many seemed to be struggling. He said that the clean air was a nectar which instilled a feeling of wellbeing, that his walks across the fields and through the woods kept him in close touch with the ground swell of life in its fullness all about. Life flowed in abundance and joy was everywhere.

I responded that it was a characteristic of man to forget despondency and bad times and to accentuate the positive. I told him that he was talking through his hat, however, when he implied that the doldrums had never touched him. His reply was, "I can remember nothing but joy and gladness in the gift of life and the experience of each day. Happiness has fallen as the morning dew and is renewed daily. I can't imagine what it would be like to be down and listless." It was later while reading his journals that the two low periods became evident, after his marriage in 1929 and when he returned home from Philadelphia. Certainly there were other lows, but these two periods were striking.

MAIL BOX

O n Needmore Road at the entrance of the long forested hallway leading to "Paradise," was his mail box, a large, metal receptacle bearing his name. This was his communications center, which received more traffic than the usual country mail box. His large volume of personal correspondence and the numerous newspapers and magazines to which he subscribed passed through this message center.

Letters arrived from all parts of the country, sometimes because of an article in a local paper about his elementary mode of existence. Others came from friends he had met on his travels or worked with across the country. Some were regular correspondents for twenty, thirty, or forty years, or until death broke the relationship. Others were from numerous local friends, setting a date for a trip with him or a visit with him at the cabin.

Neighbors and friends would leave gifts of pies, cakes, and cookies in this container. "They used to leave meat," he said, "which I had to give a decent burial in my garden where it would do some good. You can't keep meat for long in the summer time. Course, in the winter it came in right handy and was easy to keep when the weather was cold enough to preserve it." He would meet visitors, especially those who had never been to the cabin, at the mail box and walk them in to his forest glade. Often he would walk them out. Occasionally, night would fall before his guests realized how swiftly the hours passed in his company, and he would illuminate the path with an oil lantern.

His guests were of all ages and of varied interests. Scout leaders would schedule a visit and bring their boys to see his place and to talk with him. Students and teachers, the learned and the curious, came to call, to raise questions and exchange views.

If a trip was scheduled, he would meet the party at the mail box. Paul Bales said Bert always seemed to come out of the woods just as he arrived. He wondered if Bert sat in the woods until the car stopped, then walked out.

Paul reported that he went to the mail box one May day to leave a message concerning a weekend hike. There on a log sat Bert with two small boys, talking and laughing in such a festive way that Paul had a hard time breaking loose and returning to his newspaper office. "I would have given my eye teeth to have been able to remain and soak up some of the pleasure they displayed." Bert usually made two or three trips on the two-thirds of a mile path to the mail box each day. Friends and neighbors would leave messages inquiring as to his availability for a car trip or a hike or to ascertain if he would be home on a certain day so that they might come in for a visit. He would jot down an answer on a used envelope and leave it in the receptacle.

Knowing when the milkman came by, he would often go out to stop the truck and purchase a quart or two of milk.

If he was in no hurry, and he seldom was, he might sit by the box until a neighbor stopped for a talkfest. The mailmen were his friends and would pass the time of day and bring him up to date on the overnight news.

Tom Sawyer, his last mail man, arranged his schedule in order to stop at Bert's box at lunch time. Bert would often be there, and they would spend a leisurely hour in the shade in conversation. Tom said, "Bert did the talking, and I did the listening. He gave me many a pleasant hour talking about anything he wished. I remember those times with feeling. He was a delightful companion."

Tom reported that near the end Bert was getting feeble and would be tired when he came out of the woods. "He would sit down and rest. Sometimes he would take off his shoes, pull up his socks and say, 'my socks are ashamed of my ankles and keep trying to hide in my shoes.' " Bert said his mail box stood quite near the old Hawkins (Holston) boundary line. The line crossed Needmore Hill on its journey from the North Carolina border on the ridge of the Great Smoky Mountains to a spot near Kingston. This line resulted from the Holston treaty in 1791 and was surveyed by Benjamin Hawkins in 1797.

Over the years his mail box was moved several times as the rural routes were changed. It was this last box on Needmore Road that his later friends and visitors knew and which served as his principal communications center.

OF THE SAME CLOTH AS THOREAU & WHITMAN

"**G**ive me the writings of my five prophets—Thoreau, Whitman, Emerson, Burroughs,[1] and Alcott—and season with the sayings of Jesus, Jefferson, and Lincoln and let the rest go," Bert once wrote. Numerous works by and about these men lined his book shelves. The number of exemplary figures in history from whom he quoted in conversation and noted in his journals was encyclopedic. The broad span of the great received his rapt attention through seventy years of reading.

The five 'prophets' and Lincoln were all contemporaries, which denotes Bert's emphasis on nineteenth century personalities and thought. John Burroughs lived into the twentieth century, and Bert once talked with him in Florida in the early 1900s. Henry Ford, Harvey Firestone, and Burroughs were friends who often traveled together. Ford built the first, or one of the earliest, travel campers in a self-contained automotive unit fitted for cross country travel. While working temporarily in Florida as an orange picker, Bert learned that these men were camped in a nearby park. He visited their bivouac late one evening, finding Burroughs seated near a dying campfire, gazing at the heavens. The others had

---

[1] John Burroughs (1837-1921) was an American naturalist and nature essayist.

123

retired. Burroughs was a popular nature writer and philosopher, and Bert was familiar with his work. Their party had camped in the Smokies on the way South. So Burroughs and Bert talked at length about the Great Smoky Mountains.

The men most revealed in Bert were Thoreau and Whitman. When one knew him well, one could not escape knowing something of these distinct personalities, who have left a deep impression through their lives and work. By walking their individualistic paths, they were sharply marked from their contemporaries.

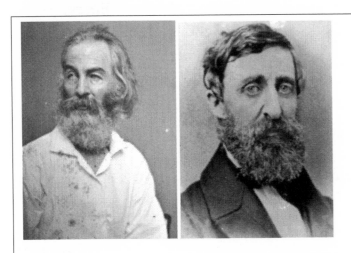

"Often I wondered whether it was Bert talking, or Whitman or Thoreau."

Bert's conversation was often laced with Thoreau or Whitman usually without reference to the source. His extensive reading and remarkable memory, reinforced by journal entries, made much that he read become a part of him. After repetition over the years, it became his own, indistinguishable from his own thought.

Often I wondered whether it was Bert talking, or Whitman or Thoreau. The message was frequently the same and sometimes the words. He embodied much of the essence of these men in his life and thought.

In the beginning of our friendship, I concluded that through his close study of their work they had been woven into the very fabric of his being. Later my conclusion shifted to the position that he used their words to voice basic concepts which he had in common with them. There was a marked difference in the men, however, for Bert lacked their creative genius.

It appeared that he found in them kindred souls who expressed lucidly in splendid language his own feelings. Thoreau wrote, "There is no more Herculean task than to think a thought about this life and then get it expressed." Their skill with descriptive imagery in flowing language placed them on a higher plane; yet Bert was quite adept in the use of the King's English, especially in conversation.

A 1945 entry in Bert's journal reads, "In Thoreau I find precedent and scripture for my own ways of living." There was never any marked change in Bert's way of life, nothing to indicate that he left off one way and switched to another. He did not abandon civilization to move to his Walden; nor did he cast off an occupation or profession to "simplify, simplify." From the beginning, he epitomized simplicity in his reflections on the essentials of meaningful existence and the material requirements necessary to fulfill the essence of life. In Thoreau and Whitman he found expression by articulate men to voice his own views and being. Bert was an incomparable man in the technological age, a keen and inquiring mind in a rustic setting, with no ambition to change his pace or setting.

Jonathan Wright, an English teacher at the Old Quaker School in Maryville, introduced Bert's English class to Thoreau in 1898. Bert was immediately captivated by this striking personality. Thoreau still fascinates students. He was fresh, enthusiastic, and attuned to nature. His unique power to record his thoughts and experiences was such that his stature increased with the passage of time. Although Thoreau was little known outside of Concord at his death in 1862 at the age of 45, his fame spread rapidly. He once said that his library consisted of a thousand books, 700 of which he had written himself. This was in reference to *A Week on the Concord and Merrimack Rivers;* 1,000 copies were published at his own expense with fewer than 300 having been sold.

"We saw so many things through the same eyes," said Bert, "that he has given me intimate and enduring companionship." It is difficult to imagine anyone existing more closely to Thoreau's way, as he lived and as he wrote, than Bert. Pick at random from Thoreau, and you will find Ole Bert revealed in one of the myriad shades of his presence. The following are a few of the illustrations from Thoreau which portray some strong feature of Herbert S. Garner in apt and accurate capsule form.

"My wealth is not possessions but enjoyment."

"A man is rich in proportion to the number of things he can afford to let alone."

"No way of thinking or doing, however ancient, can be trusted without proof."

"I enjoy more drinking water at a clear spring than out of a goblet at a gentleman's table."

"Most of the luxuries, and many of the so-called comforts, of life are not only dispensable, but positive hindrances to the elevation of mankind."

"You must live in the present, launch yourself on every wave, find your Eternity in each moment."

"What are threescore years and ten hurriedly and coarsely lived to moments of divine leisure in which your life is coincident with the life of the universe?"

Once in talking to Bert of Thoreau, I remarked, "I have come to the conclusion that in many respects you are more Thoreauvian than Thoreau himself. More than a hundred years after his death in a technological age, you live in a simpler, more primitive fashion than did he. Thoreau lived with his family in Concord. You dwell quite alone in the woods. He built his cabin at Walden Pond to face the essentials of life in order to learn what they had to teach, a two year venture. You have lived here the greater part of fifty years. In Thoreau's words, you have continuously lived 'life near the bone where it is sweetest.' This has been your permanent abode."

"Hey, I never thought of it that way. But I haven't modeled myself after him," he replied. "I have always been my own man."

"We are all the prisoners of our genes, more than we recognize." I continued. "You and Thoreau were shaped by an unusual mixture, and the similarities are many. Have you not found yourself on a completely different path from your fellows?"

"That I have," Bert replied. "They follow the paths of things and ambition and competition. Thoreau and I found that a regular job left too little time to follow our natural interests."

"You have often said also that to work six weeks a year was adequate to provide all the necessities, and did not Thoreau say the same?" I asked. "And you have expressed the thought that religion is something never spoken. That's straight from the man of Walden. One of your favorite themes is that man spends too much time paying for a home, that the price is too high in terms of work; that time can be better used; that small homes are adequate. This is also Thoreau, and there are a hundred other examples."

He laughed, "Yes, this was Thoreau. It is also, and I have come to many of his conclusions independently. Others have also made many of the same observations as Thoreau. He expressed them as well or better.

"Horace wrote, 'The more a man denies himself, the more he will obtain.' Socrates spoke in the same vein, 'The less one needs, the nearer one is to the gods.'

"Thoreau was a student of the classics. He was well-versed in Greek and Latin literature. Was this not the source of much of his basic material? Is there anything new under the sun? Any thought we have has been expressed by others and far better in most instances. I have not copied Thoreau, but I have found in him a kindred spirit."

It was Whitman's unbounded zest for life that was most reflected in Bert. From Whitman, "Each moment and whatever happens thrills me with joy;" and from Bert, "I am stepping on the stars and skimming the Milky Way." Both reveled in every shade of being and in every nuance of passing time. They bubbled with enthusiasm; they were free spirits. Whitman wrote, "What do you suppose will satisfy the soul, except to walk free and own no superior." Bert wrote, "There lives and leaps in me a love for the lowly things and a passion to be free;" and "In bellypinch I'll pay the price, but God! let me be free."

Although there were marked differences in the basic essentials, there were also marked similarities. Whitman lived in humble simplicity and wrote, "Tone yaur wants and tastes down low enough, and make much of negatives and of mere daylight and the skies." From Bert came, "There is a certain deep satisfaction in self-denial. Do away with the tinseled fripperies of life. To lighten your luggage is part of the art of living."

Postcard Text: This marks the site of his hut where he spent two and a half years writing his book "Walden or Life in the Woods." Bert's message on the reverse of this postcard: I visited Thoreau's Pond Sept. 1, 1924; and again Sept. 2, 1945.

Postcard Text: The Thoreau Room; The Antiquarian Society, Concord, Massachusetts. Bert's Message: Visited this room Sept. 2, 1945

Whitman was in gear with his age and a prophet of the future. He sang of the rising strength of his America, the throbbing mills, the humming factories, the bustling shipyards, the dynamic energy of his people. In contrast, Bert was out of tune with a later age when Whitman's America had become full grown. After visiting the assembly line of Ford Motor Company in Detroit in 1927, he expressed, "I would as leave be in Hell as to work there. Hell would be preferable, I think."

Bert began reading Whitman in 1920 while working at the Library of Congress as a guard in the rare books department and later as a gardener. From that time on Whitman was a constant and cherished companion. "Go to Whitman," said Bert, "for touch with a large soul"; and again, "To discover Whitman is to discover a new world and a new self." Bert was not a student who met the remarkable Whitman in a literature course, marveled, and moved on. He immersed and soaked himself in the vibrancy and joy flowing from Whitman which was as sparkling and invigorating as a mountain stream. He found there an essence analogous to his own, a rare heart and soul with whom he visited for the next fifty years.

As Whitman pours out himself and pictures the strength, the independence, the surging force of his people, he often depicts Bert.

> *"All forces have been steadily employ'd to complete and delight me. Now on this spot I stand*

with my robust soul." "Afoot and lighthearted I take to the open road,

Healthy, free, and the world before me,
The long brown path before me leading wherever I choose."

"Old age, flowing free with the delicious nearby freedom of death."

Whitman spent freely of his time during the Civil War visiting the sick and wounded soldiers in and around Washington and Virginia. He ran errands, wrote letters, sat with the lonely and distressed, comforted and cared for the dying. Bert knew kinship here, for he nursed the aged and the sick, worked in hospitals and sanitariums, and gave freely of his skill in caring for those approaching death in his community.

Bert wrote, "Cosmic consciousness is a third type of consciousness. First comes consciousness, then self-consciousness, then cosmic consciousness or a consciousness of the life and order of the universe. Walt Whitman reached cosmic consciousness at 34. I reached it at about 54." This reference is to an inward harmony arising from a feeling of being at one with the rhythm and flow of time and space, a meaningful part of the whole, the cosmos.

He saw in Whitman shades of the humanist. "In the center of all and object of all stands the Human Being." Whitman sang of himself and of man, lifting him to a higher level in his poetry than his accepted place in the scheme of things.

Bert visited Whitman's home in Camden on at least two occasions. He recorded in his journal in 1943, "Crossing the Delaware tonight on Camden Ferry; the moon was full and stars blazing. As I mused at the scene, Old Walt Whitman seemed near." Crossing on the ferry was often mentioned by Whitman. Walden Pond was visited by Bert September 1, 1924, and September 2, 1945, and on a third occasion.

Neither Thoreau, Whitman nor Ole Bert was concerned with the material. Theirs was a process of sharpening their senses to an absorbing alertness to all that transpired about them, whether secluded in the stillness of a soft meadow or foliaged forest, or in the company of man on busy streets. Whitman was more in unison with his compeers and spent most of his life in cities. All were excellent companions and conversationalists, giving delight in discourse, but Thoreau and Bert were more frequent seekers of solitude in the woods and fields. Words were their stock in trade, with Thoreau and Whitman being master wordsmiths.

They exercised simplicity in their actions, and it was reflected in their dress which was based on utility and comfort rather than the current fashion. They were of strong character and lived by a strict code of ethics. Truth was held in great esteem, and they had little sympathy for the false in man.

All exercised tremendous discipline in a sparse pattern of life. Each had mastered himself and saw the hours of each day utilized in efforts and leisure suited to his tastes and objectives. They kept journals recording their observations and thoughts. Thoreau was the ingenious journalist, making notes in the field and later writing and rewriting until each sentence captured his thought and reflected it clearly and concisely.

The unbounded enthusiasm which they shared was a vital key to their sparkle. Without this trait, death comes long before burial, as all observed. "Went to the funeral of Andy Jones who died thirty years ago and was bedded down today," wrote Bert.

The stoic was present in each, for they accepted life with a minimum of complaints. Bachelors they were, with Bert slipping temporarily from grace, but his nature was celibate.

Whitman and Thoreau have touched millions and will excite multitudes yet unborn. Bert touched only those with whom he came in close contact by his inimitable presence.

COMMENTS ON MAN AND THE TIMES
"SWINUS AMERICANUS"

We were walking up Chilhowee along the road to Murray Gap and Happy Valley on Bert's annual May 4th pilgrimage to Look Rock. The early morning was soft and fresh, with low clouds hanging like a cotton mantle along the crest of the mountain. The forest was showing myriad shades of tender greens, beiges, and pinks in buds and new leaves, with each species displaying its distinctive array of color.

Our attention was drawn from the elegance of the vegetation to the distraction of trash along the road. Bottles, cans, papers littered the roadside. Large deposits of garbage and appliances were piled in places.

"Swinus Americanus!" growled Bert. "I would have those filthy pigs hung by their thumbs or placed in stocks on public display or buried to the neck in their own filth. Drastic punishment, you say? No more drastic than the burden placed on the public to clear their debris. The punishment should fit the crime, and spoiling the streets and highways is a transgression against man and nature.

"Without drastic punishment they will never cease draping the landscape with their leavings. European countries don't have this problem. The streets and highways of Germany and Switzerland are spotless.

"Draw and quarter the swine, I say, and hang them in public view along the roadside to rot."

"Autobus Addictus"

"Ride and the world rides with you. Walk and you walk alone. So I walk alone. Autobus Addictus has become a disease; the auto poses a greater threat than the atomic bomb. Every time a ding-busted car passes and fills my eyes and lungs with filth and my ears with noise, I cuss so-called modern civilization. When we developed the auto for the common man, we created infinitely more problems than we solved. We became slaves of these machines. Give me a streetcar or a train; I'm allergic to cars, those noisy, polluting hunks of gas guzzling junk."

His journals make many references to the automobile. In 1923, "The auto bug seems to have bitten everyone but me." In 1928, "Autos and roads are sending this country to the dogs." In 1931 he depicted the times, "This is the age of gas and brass and jazz." He wrote in 1955, "We're expected to have 81 million cars in 1965.

Where in the Hell are we going to park 'em?" In the late sixties a neighborhood youngster came to see Bert in great distress and asked for his help. The finance company was coming out to pick up his new Thunderbird if he didn't get his delinquent payment in that day. "Well now," said Bert, "here's my advice, call them back and tell them to hurry." He never became conditioned to the automobile, nor the machine age, and considered the car the idol most worshiped in the country. "The object of most men's lives nowadays is to replace the old car with a more expensive and more gaily colored one. Folks would rather have their ass on a cushion than their feet on the ground.

"I anticipated it but never wanted to see it. I've lived too long."

Advertising

"There are few truths, only half truths, partial truths. This is evident in the great American institution of advertising. The public has been so captured by the subtle potency of repetitive advertisement that its level of discernment has been reduced to a modicum. That firm with the best pitch to the public has become the medicine man, selling its goods to the gullible—the whole American public.

"Our people have become robots to the pressures of the publicity of the sellers who have pushed them far beyond their means and their needs. Advertising is the modern con and medicine man palming off goods with a tinge of value, and an abundance of malarkey.

"It has always distressed me, this voracious worm eating our resources, leaving nothing but the pressing burden of paying and an emptiness in the belly of our being."

Progress! Bah!

"Much of what's called progress is not betterment. More often it is the speedy decay of the countryside. Progress has become synonymous with more buildings, more cars, more roads, more people, more pollution. Bah! Progress by definition is advancement to a higher or better stage.

Much of the so-called progress turns out to be the opposite— retrogression—the changing of the natural into the unnatural, the simple to the complex, the clean into the dirty, the untrampled into the trampled, the good life into the sordid, crowded and the pressed.

"You can't stop progress," they say. "Well, I say, we've got to stop progress when it means decline and not advancement."

Values

"We spend more on pet food than baby food, more on alcohol and tobacco than on education, more on movies than books, more on trash than essentials. Say! the longer I live the harder it is to understand peoples' values. Folks get what they deserve and I question whether they deserve much. They buy nothing with their time and money. No wonder they feel wasted.

"Man's sense of values should be his greatest asset. So it's easy to see that we are poverty stricken. Is a sense of value not more to be concerned with than material things?

Satisfying greeds costs more than satisfying needs."

"The main purpose of education is to acquire a sound set of values as a guide through life. We have fallen down here. This is the basis for shaping a life. To neglect this is a great betrayal, and many are those who have betrayed themselves."

Chasing the Tinsel

As we talked of the foibles and characteristics of man, we touched on one of his favorite themes. "Man is shaped by current pressures, and one of the greatest urgencies in our time is material success. So consumed are most in chasing this spurious goal that many never wake to recognize that they have blundered the greater part of living. So involved are they in the pursuit of the superfluous, in chasing the tinsel, that the finer fruits are never seen, much less picked. To be all immersed in the pursuit of a livelihood is a fatal mistake. There is more to living than this.

"Getting the bread and board of life is important, but not all consuming. The windows of our senses should be wide open. I am bathed in the tides of nature. There is beauty and fulfillment everywhere if we but slow our pace and drink it in. There is as much wonder in the land and in life as one is conditioned to appreciate, and no more."

INDEPENDENT CUSS

Bert insisted on paying his way, and each of his friends has a fund of stories to illustrate this characteristic. On occasion this trait could become a bit irritating.

Following are three sketches of personal experiences with this independent cuss.

For a time it was my practice to visit him early on Sunday mornings, when possible, and enjoy his conversation until visitors arrived. It was the only time in the week when it was certain he would be alone. I always took him a Sunday paper, and he always handed me the price of the paper, a quarter.

One Wednesday, I picked him up at his mail box for a trip to Townsend to visit the Lee Robersons. As soon as he got in the car he said, "Am I relieved to see you, I haven't slept a wink since Sunday."

"What's wrong?" I asked.

"I forgot to pay you for the paper, "and he shoved a quarter into my hand. "Now I'm square with the world, don't owe a soul." A moment later he exclaimed, "I do! I just remembered that I borrowed a penny from Dewey Simpson Saturday to buy soap, was short a penny. But I'll pay him."

"That's no cause for concern," I said, "Dewey will never let you forget it. For a man who has important things to do, you dwell too much on trivia."

"Oh, but a debt is not trivia but an obligation to be promptly honored."

"Damn!" I exclaimed, and talked about the weather.

He had asked me to take him to Gatlinburg to see Mrs. Tom Anderson, wife of the publisher of the *Tennessee Farm Journal,* with whom he had corresponded for several years but had never met. She had invited him to see her new house. For the hundredth time he asked me to stop at a service station so that he could fill the tank with gas.

"Bert, have you ever seen me place fuel in this thing?"

"Say! come to think of it, I haven't. Does it run on hot air?" "Yes, yours! Since meeting you and taking a weekly trip in this buggy with you, I haven't spent a nickel on fuel. The thing runs as smooth as silk on that gaseous hot air of yours."

"Well, I ain't going to live forever, and I owe you. You just tell me how much, and I'll be clean with the world. I can't sleep or rest if I owe."

"Well, if it'll give you peace of mind, I'll oblige you." I pulled over to the side of the road, took out my notebook and thumbed through and started scribbling. "We've been taking trips here and there for three years; and, as you know, I keep a record of everything. It so happens that I have the mileage all totaled except for today. We've traveled about 9,010 miles at 15 miles to the gallon. That comes to 600 gallons of gas. At thirty cents a gallon, that comes to exactly $180. You can give me cash or a check." He never mentioned paying for gas again.

March 21, 1970:

Because of rapidly declining health, he had been in town with his sister, Mary, and was eager to get back to the cabin to usher in Spring in his woods. I had contacted him the day before and learned that he was going back to the cabin the next day and needed wood for his stove. I told him that I would bring my chain saw out after work and cut what he needed.

"No!" he said, "I won't let you do that!"

"Why not," I asked in surprise, "I need the exercise."

"No!" he repeated, "I pay for what I get. I'll hire a man."

"OK, you can hire me. How about a dollar an hour?" He accepted that.

A hickory was down within fifty feet of the front of the cabin, and I began cutting it into short lengths for his old stove.

He sat on the front stone step in his bare feet. Just as I got into the work, it began to drizzle. He urged me to come in, but the shower was no bother, and I continued to saw.

He called several times telling me I would catch my death. Finally I said, "Bert, dammit, leave me be. I carry this twelve pound saw and a can of gas three-fourths of a mile in and I'll have to carry it out. I've been sawing for 12 minutes. Now at a dollar an hour that comes to twenty cents. I always knew you were tight, but never knew just how tight."

After that outburst he let me finish the job which took no more than half an hour. Nor did he mention paying me, but gave me his old copy of *The Education of Henry Adams.* So the payment far exceeded the agreed on price for my labor.

THE HERENESS OF THE THERE

July 14, 1968

We had leisurely walked the three miles up the ridge from Rich Gap to the top of Cerulean Knob on which sits the Rich Mountain fire tower in a lush patch of grass. We talked of this and that, in Bert's terms "the hereness of the there, the wentness of the gone, and the whichness of the what. "We had paused occasionally for huckleberries.

I had learned from many conversations with my friend that he discoursed on two levels. His normal conversation was off the top of his head, with no great depth but a delightful chatter about any subject. He would skip from topic to topic. The other level was of greater depth and often revealed the underlying current of his thought. He was bubbling over in high spirits, saying, "I'm intoxicated with the wine of life. Sometimes I get plumb drunk with it."

Often we talked about various subjects of philosophy, and I wished to delve deeper into specifics to get a better understanding of his mature and seasoned metaphysics. So I began by asking his thoughts based on a lifetime of reading, study, and conversation, on the origin of matter or substance. Was there a beginning or first cause?

"Well, you want to start at the bottom, do you, for you have gone to the heart of it. When was the beginning and what was before and when is the end and what after?

"The foundation of the universe is matter and matter is energy. It is the material of which the cosmos is constructed. Matter and energy, according to the Law of the Conservation of Mass, is indestructible. The elements in one form or another have existed always and will go on existing forever. Followed to its logical conclusion, I arrive at the knowledge that there was no beginning nor will there be an end. It was here, always here, always changing, and to remain here throughout eternity. Yes, we are star stuff, and have no way of knowing how many times the elements of our bodies have been in different forms in stars and in the clouds of space dust in evolving stellar forms.

"Everything—man, earth, and the vastness of time and space, are all parts of nature; that grand, mysterious, endless spectre of which we are aware of only an infinitesimal part.

"I've talked with you about my philosophy instructor and good friend in Philadelphia, David Arnold," Bert said as he took a book from his shoulder satchel. "He is now deceased, and his wife sent me several copies of his recent book, *You of Nature*." He read the following poetic prose from the first page:

> *"Cosmos—you cannot escape me—no limits have you, but neither has science and mind! Swift are your pelletstars—but mind can overtake them! Your multiplicity, agelessness, omnipotence, resplendence, boundlessness staggered me but I*

*have recovered and encompassed you! An
omnipresent atom you are—your galaxies the
photons! Elementary energy cannot be nullified—
and all matter is energy. Within totality I witness
'dead' and expiring Earthly and Celestial things
and am saddened, but momentarily only, for all
cessation is but pause for energetic reconstitution.
With embryo and infant suns and planets Your
nurseries overflow.*

*"Verily, you would deceive, your 'stars' upon
inspection (beyond fellow Milky Way's suns—)
are actually entire galaxies! (some visible with
naked eye)—each consisting of sun-moon-planet-
nebula-comet—millions—similar to our galaxy.
Behold— each complete system turns—vast
stellar merry-go-rounds—so immense that they
require 370 million years for average galactic
rotation. And Earthlings have insufficient
numbers to count your galaxies!"*

"Marvelous!" I said, "Arnold was a talented wordsmith
to have shaped such a portrait of the cosmos. Also he
expressed great optimism on the reach of the mind,
which has stretched with the advance of astronomy
and physics."

Bert was into his subject, and continued, "The whole
process is one of evolution in which a million years is
but an instant. The age of the earth is now accepted as
being in the rough neighborhood of four or five billion
years—a mite more ancient than the 6,000 years as
promulgated by churchmen. When the Park Service
put the sign up in Cades Cove stating the limestone of
the Cove was laid down 300,000 years ago, John

Oliver said, 'That will have to come down; the earth was formed only 6,000 years ago.' The sign remained.

"Man and all that we know is the product of this constant change through evolution. Leakey in his Olduvai Gorge search established man or his fore-bearers in Africa more than a million years back. So we have been evolving from the most simple form of life for a billion or more years. We are not the ultimate in man. Hopefully, we can control the environment so that we may continue to evolve and not go the way of the dinosaur and hosts of other forms which failed to endure. Man too can become extinct through the natural process and more rapidly through thoughtless care of his space base. Yet, with careful control of the environment as far as is within our means, we can be around for a million more years. Viewing the technological progress in the past 400 years, what can't we accomplish in future eons? I say that the science fiction writers in their wildest imaginations haven't touched the marvels of future scientific advances if we successfully shape ourselves and our resources for a lengthy existence."

I questioned him on his thoughts of intelligent life in the reaches beyond.

"Space is replete with the basic materials for life which evolves when given a favorable environment and time. Intelligent life is not only possible, but extremely probable, on millions of other planets throughout the depths of space. Man, or his intelligent likeness, is out there in all stages of development; in states ranging from the earliest form to far superior beings than we imagine."

It was noon and we paused for lunch. His meals were always simple. Today it consisted of cheese and crackers, a tomato, and a grapefruit. As he peeled the tomato, he remarked, "Nature wraps its fruits in sanitary packages; thank goodness it ain't cellophane."

A pileated woodpecker flew across the clearing in undulating flight, crow size with red topknot, black body with white wing streaks, a beautiful winged wood driller. The prosaic name of woodhen didn't do him justice, and we called him the 'Lord God bird' as he is known in some areas.

Bert said, "That bird is literally made of dust as you and I, and that dust in what ever shape or form is star stuff."

After lunch, we continued, moving closer to the "Hereness of the There." Bert continued, "From substance and matter, and time and space, although we have only skimmed the surface, we come home to man and his place in the void. This has been the bone most chewed by philosophers as well as ordinary men. I have often nibbled it around the edges but never got as good a bite as I wanted, and that seems true of most.

"We are here in the present, given an intelligence which is often ill-used or ignored. The myth of Adam relates how he was expelled from the Garden of Eden for eating of the Tree of Knowledge. For that sin, he came to live on the earth as we know it. It has always bumfoozled me that men have so long accepted this story as the act of the original sin. Intelligence and reason were given a slap in the face from the beginning. Is man not to use that one trait which

150

separates and elevates him above other animals? He has been slapped down time and again by church and state for arriving at logical conclusions through the use of his far-ranging mind.

"Galileo had to stop writing and teaching of his telescopic observations which proved the Copernican theory that the earth and planets revolved around the sun. Spinoza, that gentle intellect, was ostracized and excommunicated from his church and declined to publish his finest work, *Ethics*, for fear of the consequences. So the brilliant book came to light after his death. The State of Tennessee long outlawed the teaching of evolution. The examples of such treatment of good and intelligent men and ideas throughout recorded history reveals the resistance of bodies of authority to enlightenment and to the destruction of cherished tradition, regardless of how fraught with error.

"We are becoming more tolerant, but that stigma of intolerance still characterizes man and his institutions. What benefits we could enjoy could we but eradicate this black plague. If we were but to use the brains at our disposal in the field of ethics and education to deal with this and other problems, we would make giant strides as we did when we turned our scientists toward the moon.

"Yet, man is more difficult to scientifically probe in all aspects of his being than is moon space. The social sciences are moving forward, and perhaps, when our attention is fully focused on the social good, we will unlock many doors which will lead to alleviating the social evils of which intolerance is but one."

"Bert, for an old reprobate you do a fair job of putting your thoughts together when hard pushed," I said. "Now let's talk about man and his place in the scheme of things. Does nature show him any preference?" "Yes and No. YES, she has given us the gift of mind and NO, she pays no more attention to us than yonder piss ant. Her forces of destruction, the wind, the rain, the waves, the thunderbolts and the quakes pay us no nevermind and rumble on in their disasters. Yet, the mind permits us to plan to a degree to offset the damage wrought by these events. We build dykes or move to higher ground. We are informed of pending tornadoes and hurricanes and take protective measures."

"Many animals have a sixth sense by which they seem to be forewarned and are able to seek shelter from natural forces such as storms," I remarked. "What about the sixth sense of man, extrasensory perception which is now receiving considerable study?" He answered, "I have reached no conclusion on this subject other than, whatever it is, it is a natural sense which scientific research will reveal eventually to be or not to be. I flat don't know the final answer."

"What is the purpose of man?" I asked.

"Ah, well now, that's a loaded question. I'll begin by telling you what it ain't; it is not to exalt God and glorify Him forever. The fellow who came up with that was way off his rocker. No real or imaginary, unselfish omnipotence would desire such adulation for Himself and such a void purpose for man.

"The purpose of man is to measure up to his potentialities, to use what he has within himself and in his environment to shape a good life for himself and all men. It's as simple as that."

And we talked of life after death. . . .

Bert said, "We are slowly discarding the illusion of immortality which someone aptly described as a 'brainwoven conceit.' Given an intellect, we must follow the path of reason rather than that of our longings and blind faith.

"I attribute the longing for life beyond the grave to many things among which are the unfulfilled life, man's concept of himself as godlike, the brief life span, and the strong instinct for survival.

"Men have often led drab and slavelike existences, experiencing dire privation and suffering. The vision of an existence beyond this type of reality has had great appeal and has softened and soothed his harsh life when he thought of it as a temporary preparation for fulfillment and endless bliss beyond this realm of being. It softens also the shock of men dying in their prime, or the death of children when one views a continued life in another state of being. I have found less enthusiasm for eternity in the old whose bodies and minds are worn out. They are tired and ready for the endless sleep.

"Man has pictured himself as the center of all things and the reason for the earth and the sky and the whole of the universe; he has magnified himself into that which he is not. With such a view of himself, he easily accepted the idea of immortality as his destiny. He does experience some difficulty, however, in depicting this future life.

153

"The drive for life is deeply ingrained in every fiber of our being and in the unconscious; and this leads to a yearning for a future existence, and in some religions into a belief in past life.

"Yet, I cannot imagine an eternity of being, especially for the fellow who doesn't know how to occupy his time on a Sunday afternoon. For me, there is only this one life. Treasure every moment; life passes as quickly as the blinking of an eye.

"Man should accept with delight the absence of future life, for based on my observations a heavy majority would end up in hell, burning. So the absence of immortality should be a welcome relief rather than a disappointment.

"Life is here; life is now; and it should be lived with that understanding. Most people live this way, and then double-talk about a future existence just in case there is one.

"There is enough for man to do to provide fulfilling existence for the benefit of himself and others, now and in the future. The warm sun, the splendid earth, the myriad array of wonders about us are ours to enjoy. Problems, yes, but they are our problems and will be mastered by us.

"There is little evidence of immortality, only desire and faith. Thoreau said, 'Let us take one world at a time.' This is the only world over which we have the slightest bit of control. This is the only life over which we exercise any influence. I have lived with this in mind.

"Is it not far more virtuous to live a moral life without a carrot before us as an incentive than to shape our lives because of the prospects of the reward of heaven?

"Although all the answers are not in, evolution fits what we know of the history of life and of stellar bodies and the story of matter in its changing forms. When we know that stars are being born and dying after a life of some ten billion years, immortality for men leaves me cold."

Bert's conversation to this point had amplified some features of his philosophy of Humanism, and I asked if he would boil it down for a layman to understand; he answered with:

"It is difficult to put into a few words an idea which is not completely covered in any book.

"Humanism is a man-centered philosophy which is quite old and largely unrecognized by the name of Humanism. It goes all the way back to Protagoras in the Fifth Century B.C. who wrote 'Man is the measure of all things.' Corliss Lamont's book, *The Philosophy of Humanism*, is the best treatment of the subject to date.

"In this system of thought the keys are man, nature, reason, science, and democracy. Man is of first concern, with the clear goal of happy, productive, and useful lives for all man in our natural setting. Man depends on man and calls upon the full strength of his science and reason to shape his present and his future. Democracy is essential as the social and political environment for humanism. It requires an open society for the full range of free expression of ideas and civil liberties.

"It is diametrically opposed to the thought expressed by St. Augustine, 'Cursed is everyone who places his hope in man.' For all the hopes of humanism are in man and his abilities to master himself and his environment."

I interrupted here to ask, "Have we not moved away from expecting the supernatural to fight our secular battles for us?"

"Yes, from every practical standpoint; but there remains a cloud of confusion to be cleared. This cloud lingers from old beliefs in the supernatural, in predestination, in universal determinism, and in fatalism. Too many accept that the problems we face are preordained and the way things were meant to be, put upon us by a higher authority who handles us as puppets on a string so that we cannot change what is.

"This religious, deterministic philosophy must be cast off; and man must accept that the fault is with him and not the gods. He creates his own heaven or hell. Have him accept the full responsibility for his actions and his destiny for the blights he fosters on himself and let him not curse the darkness.

"That is the kernel of humanism; a philosophy that I believe is superior to all others and with which all men can and should live in harmony, one with another, across all boundaries.

"It will be a difficult task to bring about, but the longest journey begins with the first step. And this is the first step for an enlightened tomorrow.

"It is simple and straightforward, devoid of hocus pocus. It is open to change when reason and science dictates.

"Let me summarize," I said, "to see if I follow you. Your philosophy denies the supernatural; it denies immortality; it places man in an evolving, changing nature of which he is the highest product. The burden and the joy of life is here and now. If he marshals his talents and arrays them against his problems, he will shape his life on the highest order and mold his environment for a long and happy future. Is that correct?"

"That's the way of it," he answered.

"How many of your neighbors have you converted to humanism?" I asked.

"None. I haven't tried. They are too steeped in tradition, and tradition holds fast. But I see their youngsters challenging on their own, questioning and casting off that which doesn't stand close scrutiny.

"The future is in our youth; they are our most valuable resource. I am not always impressed by their ethics which we handed to them, but I am delighted that they are breaking free of religious tradition, to question, to think, and to learn what was wrong with the fettering chains of the past. My hope goes with them for an enlightened tomorrow with complete tolerance for all men and thought."

I observed, "You spoke of democracy being necessary for the philosophy of humanism, a setting in which man can freely express diverse thoughts and views. You implied that tolerance is essential. Yet our system hasn't developed such an open society in almost two hundred years, nor has any political body brought man to a reasonable level of tolerance. I see no immediate hope that our neighbors will be more open and accepting of conflicting views in the near future. Some of the tenets of your beliefs would be anathema to the closed mind and to all fundamentalists. The Bill of Rights grants free speech, and the Constitution separates church and state.

"Haven't you encountered opposition and intolerance to your off-brand way of living and your ideas?"

"Yes. I have been cussed and preached at and sent straight to hell many times," he answered and continued.

"I have often been shocked and disappointed by the bigot convinced that his was the only way and that those who disagreed are damned. Man's intolerance to man has shaped all history. For an informed people we are not very enlightened.

"I have experienced intolerance because of my manner of living—alone and off the beaten path. My conversation often revealed thoughts contrary to established beliefs and traditions. In earlier days my views raised many a brow and set in motion many a reproaching tongue. The situation has changed, however. I have either outlived them, or they have come to accept me.

"I have never escaped the wonders of youth. Every day brings something new and enticing to titillate me. Age has not diminished my mental powers. There are tremendous reservoirs of competence and knowledge in many of retirement age if we would but harness this resource." The sun had moved past the midpoint of the western sky, turning from a ball of fire to one of soft cotton behind a veneer of clouds. We left that enticing spot and went down the trail conversing in a lighter vein, with Bert spilling off from Omar Khayyam. The following quatrain stuck in my mind as most appropriate for our switch in conversation.

"But leave the wise to wrangle, and with me
The Quarrel of the Universe let be:
And, in some corner of the Hubbub coucht,
Make Game of that which makes as much of
thee."

LAST CAMP OUT

June 18 & 19, 1969

Dewey Simpson suggested that we take Bert on an overnight trip to the mountains. We were concerned that his health would soon forbid such outings. Dewey checked with Flickinger or Mynatt (his doctors) and the plan was approved, if Bert was willing.

Bert welcomed the opportunity when we informed him of the destination. The Mt. Collins shelter is located only a half mile off the Clingman's Dome Road, perfectly situated for our purpose. Bert advised that he didn't like the wire mesh bunks, "They make a checker board pattern on my arse." We told him he could sleep on the ground. "I'll do it," he said, "or put a mattress of leaves on the bunk."

As we drove into Gatlinburg, Bert growled, "Lordamercy! just look at it. They've built on every inch of space. Why, the shops and motels ain't got room to breathe. But it draws people like molasses draws flies.

"Now the folks in Townsend can't wait till they ruin Tuckaleechee Cove. They want more buildings, more people, more cars till they're running over each other. You know what I'd like to do, I'd buy Townsend if I had the dough and give it back to the Cherokees.

"Say! it's a sight in this world to see the Indians skinning the whites in Cherokee. It's about time too; we skinned them of everything they had. An Indian dresses in a fancy headdress, never used by the old Cherokees, poses with fotchon folks (tourists) for a picture and charges good money too. They sell Cherokee trinkets made in Taiwan. Yes sir, it's a pure pleasure to watch 'em skinning the whites. More power to 'em, I say.

"You know, we could pay off the national debt with the money folks spend for trash."

Driving up the steep grade to Newfound Gap, we touched on fasting, as a means of protesting policy and conditions, recently in the news.

"Hey! I've fasted many a time. Sometimes I was out of grub but more often to clean my system. It's recommended in the Bible and practiced in some religions. This fellow from Knoxville often visits and tells me after fasting seven days he sees visions. He says the visions are often fantastic. I tell him anybody will see visions after going without food for a week. If you go longer, you're liable to see most anything.

"Now I recommend that our youth fast for their highs, it's a lot cheaper than drugs, I'll tell you that."

We parked at the Spruce Fir Nature trail. Our offer to carry his knapsack and bedding was refused—as expected.

On approaching the shelter, we experienced disappointment as a dozen scouts and two leaders were settling in. We considered going to the Davenport

Gap shelter, but decided to rig a tent of plastic sheeting. A large piece of plastic and rope had been left by recent campers.

Later, as we walked to the spring, Bert pointed to a gnarled, grotesque tree and asked, "You know what that tree is?"

Dewey said it was probably a spruce or fir. "Nope, that's a democrat tree, crooked and rotten clean through."

"And that's a republican tree, I suppose," said Dewey, pointing to a majestic fir.

"Now you're learning," said Bert, "you can learn more in these here mountains than you can in universities. I thought you boys knew your trees."

"We do," replied Dewey, "we just never took politics from Professor Garner."

As Dewey and I cooked dinner, Bert visited with the scouts, who couldn't believe this old man was camping out. Bert returned with a half gallon of milk and reported that this was a food drop for the scouts and they were overloaded with milk and eggs. We were pleased to learn that they would make an early departure on the morning.

Dewey and I had told Bert we were bringing the food for all. We prepared steak and potatoes, and he declined to share. Instead, he pulled out a peanut butter sandwich and consumed it and the milk.

As we ate, I brought to Bert's attention a brightly colored caterpillar climbing his trouser leg. "This feller's a friend of mine, and he's welcome to travel where he will. I don't kill anything, not even flies. 'Course they don't hang around my place. They would starve to death." Around two a.m. the heavens opened, and a relentless downpour battered our flimsy shelter. Soon water was penetrating from several places. Our sleeping bags became wet, and we maneuvered about seeking dry spots. We considered going into the shelter cabin, building a fire, and sitting it out. We faulted Dewey for the inadequate protection from the elements.

We talked of the savage storm experienced two years before on Spence Field with Paul Bales, Roy Crawford and a couple others. The blasts of wind had shaken the shelter with explosive power. Rain and hail had come in driven sheets, pounding the metal roof like a running army of ball peen hammers. In comparison to that experience, this was little more than a drizzle.

So we remained where we were and encouraged Bert to reel off Omar Khayyam to put us to sleep. He obliged with stanza after stanza, followed by "When nothing else works, you try philosophy." He capped this off with a timely quote, "Even this shall pass away," referring to our uncomfortable state.

As Dewey and I were dozing off, he boomed, "Say! I couldn't sleep with you fellows on a clear night; so why should I blame the rain."

We crawled out around seven in a dense fog which was moving eastward. The scouts were hustling up their grub and making ready to depart. They left before eight, and we were relieved to have what we had anticipated—the mountain top to ourselves. Bert ambled around in the enveloping cloud, and came out with, "Say! this is as fresh and clean as all outdoors." Dewey and I marveled at the resilience and humour of our eighty-three year old companion who needed nothing, wanted nothing, to be fool happy anywhere, anytime.

Later he told us, "I don't feel as well here as at home. Oldsters have a degree of hardening of the arteries which is hampered somewhat by the elevation. It's about 6,000 feet here."

The scouts had left two gallons of milk and several dozen eggs. We recovered from the night's ordeal with eggs, bacon, sausage, coffee and milk. Bert declined to share our bounty, except the milk, and leisurely finished off a half gallon with his peanut butter sandwich.

At nine o'clock the sun peeped through; and by eleven the sky had cleared.

In the meantime we were entertained by chipmunks scampering about like characters from Disney. A raven flew over and greeted us with harsh croaks. Juncos flitted about searching for crumbs. A boomer, red squirrel, shattered the stillness.

Dewey placed a couple of eggs on the ground to see how the chipmunks would handle them. They pushed them about, turned them on end, fussed and fumed till they finally cracked them, then cavorted in pleasure at their success.

He then worked on a milk carton and explained that he was trying to figure a way to make a trap, like a small rabbit trap, to catch a chipmunk. He told of trapping muskrats as a boy in Middle Tennessee. Bert told him his head had too many holes in it.

About the time Dewey gave up on the trap, we had a nosey visitor. A medium sized bear came to the edge of the clearing, sniffed, and slowly moved toward us.

Bert and I sat quietly. The next thing we knew, Dewey came out of the cabin with the rope used to string up the tent. "What are you doing now?" we asked. He was making a loop in the rope, and replied, "I'm going to lasso me a bear." We told him he was crazy as a loon. He insisted, and said it would help if we got behind the bruin and forced him toward him. He was swinging the loop over his head, testing it.

Bert: "I'm agin messing with that feller; looks like he's hankering to mess with us. "

Dewey: "If you'll help me, I'll get him."

Bert: "Well now, what you plan to do with him when you catch him? "

Dewey: "I haven't figured that out yet. "

Bert: "We don't want no bear roaming the Smokies with you in his belly and a rope round his neck. He'll have an awful bellyache and is liable to choke if that rope snags."

Dewey: "Aren't you going to help me? "

Bert: "Nope! I ain't gonna tell Gertrude (Dewey's wife) yu wuz et by a bar; Woody'll have to do that."

Shortly, we chased the bear away, despite Dewey's protests, and passed on to more serious topics.

We talked of the disenchantment of youth with many institutions, of the breakdown of morals. We wondered if our present form of government could master the art of governing our complex society.

We questioned whether the system of elected representatives in Washington would long survive. The energies of the legislators seemed centered on staying in office. To do so they must get the votes. To get votes they continue draining the resources with pork barrel projects and questionable giveaway programs. The conclusion was that you can't get efficient and effective legislation from five hundred politicians lusting for a place in the sun when they should be concentrating on the benefit of the nation as a whole.

We touched on the Vietnam War and the staggering drain of men and resources. We decided after a couple of hours of viewing the nation's problems that it was far more fun to lasso a bear. So we moved to lighter conversation as we packed and moved out. Bert told us that he was an accomplished loafer, and Dewey and I gave him no argument.

He said, "A lot of folks say I never pulled my weight, and they are right. I've gone my own way, done my own thing; and I wouldn't have changed it for the world. Everyone looks at the world through his own knothole, and I like the slant of mine." As we approached Gatlinburg, Bert said, "If it's all right with

you, let's miss Gatlinburg
and take the Little River
Gorge road through
Townsend."

EXCERPTS FROM THE LAST JOURNAL (1969-70)

1969

Mar. 9th: At 6:45 Dr. Tom Holder and Inez Burns came for me at Mary's and to Dr. Beulah Kittrell's at Louisville for an intellectual feast as well as a banquet of good eats. Dr. Mynatt and wife there. Dr. Kittrell has a fine library of good books—many historical.

20th: Dewey and Woody came to Harper Library at 1 p.m. for me and to my woods to spend the rest of day and I spent the night and the next day and night. When I got into my woods on the first glorious day of Spring, I felt my soul expand.

27th: One of my impediments through life has been that I have picked up too many friends.

28th: At home in high glee and muchly en rapport. A perfectly clear day—little wind and sky blue with mts. clear. Went to mailbox 3 times today. The setting sun tonight peeped around the N. side of my big dogwood the clothes line has been tied to for 49 years.

April 2nd: The entries in a personal journal should be kept terse and distilled.
The pitiful thing is not that some people can't see the sun rise and set, it is that they are unable to value these great shows.

16th: My religion—Humanism—lifts me above the sordid things of this life and into the higher realms of pure being.
My soul shriveled a bit in Oklahoma and Kansas—2 yrs.—in spite of the open prairies—there were no mountains.

27th: The process of education consists in clearing oneself of a number of foolish presumptions, humbugs, and prejudices that beset the common man's mind.
Lin Yutang

May 4th: Perfect weather. Met Carson Brewer and wife Alberta at my mailbox at 9 a.m. Woody was already there. To Allegheny Hotel site in Carson's car. Left car at Johnny Bishops and hiked to hotel site and on to Yellow Sulphur. Back to Bishops and in car around to Blair Spring. Owen Downey there. Lunch at Blair

Spring.
I have come to the conclusion that
the luxuries of this world are hum
bug and the idea that they are
essential to happiness is a most
magnificent absurdity. Sidney
Lanier—Written at Montvale Springs

8th: When I get in my good easy chair that my
two fine doctors gave me, the world
can go hang.

11th: Doctor, you won't catch old Bert feeling
sorry for himself—elation holds
more joy.
Many philosophers come to my
woods to talk out life's problems.
Men or women can't hypnotize me.
Only Nature or beauty touches my
emotions.

20th: I am now absorbing in luxurious ease
every moment of this glorious
springtime—probably my last.

June 1st: Dewey came and to his house in Maryville
for a grand lunch. Mrs. Simpson is a
first class cook. To Jones Bend to
see Bertha. Dewey and I hiked
through the honeysuckles to the old
tumbled down Jones homestead.
Back by Harry Proffitt's fish farm
that Dewey designed. Dewey fotch
me to Fairview Grocery. Visited on
home with Paul Bales and Minnie

Kidd and Susie Weeks. Over the
ridge home from Tom Baughs.

7th: Was to go to Victor Simpson's wedding this
p.m. at Alcoa M. E. Church but was
not up to it. In my 84 yrs. have
never seen a wedding.
There is something vulgar about
parading ones naked emotions.

8th: The fore part of our lives cannot be as
rewarding as the latter because we
are not mature enough to value it.
I am constantly reminded of my vast
ignorance.

11th: At whippoorwill dawn and dusk I have a
sort of spiritual illumination or
mental awareness.

14th: Contentment is one of my favorite words—
tranquility is another.
I don't see well nor hear well nor
think well but I laugh well.

18th: Woody came for me at 1 p.m. at mailbox—
picked up Dewey at Woody's house.
To the Collins Gap Shelter and
found 14 Ohio people there—so we
had to sleep on the bosom of mother
earth in a drizzly all night rain with
only a borrowed piece of plastic over
us. I had to use my bread for a
pillow to keep the bears from getting
it. They circled around all night. The
Ohio people left early next morning

for Fontana leaving the shelter with
fireplace to us. We had a roaring fire
and Woody and Dewey cooked a
feast of T-bone steak, eggs, coffee,
etc. etc. Dewey fixed a rope to lasso
a bear that pestered, but bruin
lunged at him and Dewey
retreated—so did Bruin.
I am walking, tottering leisurely and
happily toward the sunset.

29th: I am simply fading away—happy as any
fool.

July 2nd: I haven't much future left, but—Oh! what a
past!

20th: The articles written about Ole Bert miss
the substance of his life. He lives a
very deep spiritual life close to
Nature which is the source of all life
and being.

22nd: One of the most astounding things in this
silly world is the gullibility of
mankind.
Man, the fool rascal, has an
inveterate capacity for superstition,
aberrations, hallucinations,
delusions and a tendency to fall
down and worship something he
knows not of—the supernatural.
One purpose of Zen is to clear the
mind of delusions and rubbish that
have been planted there.

Aug. 5th: Don't feed spiritual hunger with a chemical diet of drugs and liquor.

7th: This little spasm we call life has been a hilarious event for me. Still I look forward with keen anticipation to its termination.

10th: I'm in a predicament—too damned lazy to live and too busy to die. Living alone here in my ancestral woods, I can do my own thing to perfection. Who else can do this? I know of no one.

17th: Woody met me at mailbox at 8—to his Millers Cove farm for a circus with the Earl Franklins. Robbed W's bees—got a big lot of honey. Woody gathered corn and cantaloupes. I cut his okra, picked his beans and tomatoes. We then took Earl to his dads—old Bill F. 83 near Coker Hill. Thence we 4—old Bill, Earl and W. and I took off for Walland and got on the new Foothills Parkway and followed it to its end near the Sevier Co. line. Back tracked and up the old Townsend Rd. to old Barefoot Jerry Effler's store. Jerry went to school to me 62 yrs. ago at College Hill. He fiddled and danced for us and we had a frolic, drawing a crowd. Up Carr's Creek to Frogtown Rd. and back to old Bill Franklins. Took Earl home to Millers Cove then Woody and I took off for Dewey S.,

174

Maryville to take him a lot of honey
and cantaloupes. Mrs. Simpson
served us refreshments proper and
she gave me a whole big cake to
take home. I split it in the middle
and made Woody take half of it.
Back to my mailbox and to Young's
to get my Sunday paper. A big day—
all around.

24th: "To dream the impossible dream
　　　To fight the unbeatable foe
　　　To bear the unbearable sorrow
　　　To run where the brave dare not go
　　　To right the unrightable wrong
　　　To be better far than you are
　　　To try when your arms are too weary
　　　To reach the unreachable star.
　　　This is my quest."
　　　Don Quixote in *Man of La Mancha*

31st: At 83 ¾ a man has a license to be
　　　crotchety.
　　　I can never forgive the church for its
　　　treatment of such nonconformists
　　　as Emerson, Thomas Paine, Robert
　　　Ingersoll and Thoreau and
　　　Whitman.

Sept. 6th: For the raucous TV—squawk box—I have
　　　only the utmost loathing.

7th: Of the 83 Summers I have lived on this
　　　mundane sphere this one of 1969
　　　has been the happiest and the most
　　　worthwhile.

9th: The highest human good is human happiness. Happiness for self and for others. Humanist

13th: Morality springs from philosophy not from religion.
Schweitzer
Most people are incapable of looking the cockeyed world straight in the eye.

21st: My trouble seems to be overexuberance. Is this spiritual awareness?
Man will hug a delusion much closer than the truth.
I have explicit faith in the infinitude of the universe. I doubt its goodness or its evil.

23rd: Death cannot hurt us in the least; it is only in life that we suffer.

Oct. 2nd: This date just 60 years ago I took off from my birthplace to "go west young man"—to beard the cockeyed world. Landed in Chicago, then St. Paul and Seattle. Finally in Los Angeles. Oh! those 60 years.

4th: It is strange that my morale and euphoria is so much higher at 84 than at 24 or 34 or 44.

23rd: Woody fotch at 1:30 p.m. Mr. Don Whitehead and Saul Pett of N.Y., two noted literary characters, to discuss the sorry world and the silly rat race we are in. We talked a lot about world affairs, but we actually settled nothing. The sick cockeyed world is going to Hell in a hack.

Nov. 2nd: Content much of the day just to sit and watch the falling autumn leaves and see the glorious day go by.

16th: Living today in the lap of luxury on the leavings of the hilarious party we had here last night. A gay party— those present—Sen. Roy Crawford, Tom Click—undertaker but didn't need him, Gene Hamilton and Paul Bales of *Maryville Times*, Woody Brinegar, Dan Lawson, Dr.'s Mynatt and Flickinger— needed them, Victor Simpson, Dewey S.—creator and dispenser of the drinks. His crime list was long—largely mead—a honey drink. The wine and the conversation flowed and scintillated but everyone stayed sober. This a.m. the floor was covered with goober hulls and other debris. The food was goobers with cheese and crackers. The crackers were all over the floor too this a.m. Lunch out on the stump—still leftovers from last night—in the bright sun and still at temp. of 52.

27th: Perhaps—maybe the word effete
(exhausted with age) tells my tale.

28th: I like to hear my fire talk to me—and it
shore does.
Let me die, laughing. No sighing o'er
past sins; they are forgiven. Spilled
on this earth are the joys of heaven.
Let me die. LAUGHING.
Wintering in St. Petersburg, Florida

Dec. 28th: Life was never more worthwhile to me than
those last days of December 1969—
now in my 85th year—and going
strong.

29th: Read in M. Lake Library much of day. Sat
on Mirror Lake bench a while and
gassed a fine old man (85) from
Nebraska. He spends his summers
in St. Pete too.
A woman came and sat by us—
somewhat "fricked in the coop"—She
told me after the man left that I
should shave my whiskers.

1970

Jan. 6th: It's raining rain this a.m. and I'm reading
and writing in my room. Ate my
breakfast in room on stashed away
grub. To Philosophy Class in p.m.

13th: My mind expands continually without
drugs and I can detect no

deterioration except failing memory.
I have a perfect right to be crotchety.

18th: Sat in Williams Park for 2 hrs., 10 to 12 in
a reverie— not trance but
transported, transfused, bemused,
and translated.
Life vibrates for me almost a
constant harmonious note.

19th: I'm on a "trip" herein St. Pete—a drugless
"trip"—constantly "high" on the wine
of life.
In my woods, also in St. Pete I reach
out and grab life—here I have it by
the neck.

20th: I've had some pain in my neck for the past
3 days— probably too much
rubbernecking.
Dammit—I took a Fla. vacation to
get away from people, and here in
St. Pete I got right into bed with
humanity—a lot of them.
When a man has shed his illusions,
delusions and indoctrinations, he
also sheds his egotism.

21st: Too cool and windy to sit in Park this a.m.
so I wrote letters in my room and
read a good part of JOB from the
Gideon's Bible.
"If I say I will forget my complaint, I
will leave off my heaviness and
comfort myself." Job 9:27
"Naked came I out of my mother's

womb (Nature) and naked shall I
return thither." Job 1:22
"What is man that thou shouldest
magnify him?" Job 7:17 "As the
cloud is consumed and vanisheth
away; so he that goeth down to the
grave shall come up no more." Job
7:9
"If a man die, shall he live again."
Job 14:10

23rd: This is Mother's birthday, 121st. Got a lot
of letters today. Lunch in room,
avocados, milk, doughnuts, apple
juice. Supper on end of pier with the
screaming gulls. They cuss me and I
cuss them—windy.
At my age it is surely not much sin
to take one cup of coffee at
breakfast.
I have a rendezvous with death.

25th: I like to cater a bit to my own
whimsicalities.
I've had more fun poking fun at
homo sapiens here in Fla. than a
cage of monkeys.

26th: Age loosens an old man's tongue and
empties his mind.

Feb. 15th: The brave man carves out his fortune, and
every man is the son of his own
works. Don Quixote Life has to be
lived largely in terms of effort.
"I charge thee fling away ambition;

by that sin fell the angels."
Shakespeare
As of now I have not matured and
most likely never will. He noblest
lives and noblest dies who makes
and keeps his self-made laws.
The Rubaiyat has been to me a
source of solace and unfailing
satisfaction.

Mar. 8th: Death is no mystery—life is.

15th: Christianity won't help one iota when the
"Reaper" comes. He is not "Grim" to
me—He is welcome.
Life has always been rather a joke
with me. Death will be no joke but it
will be good—it will be release.

April 5th: I will meet and greet death with the same
fortitude I use in meeting life.
Life is more worthwhile to me now
than when I first took the job.

10th: A perfect day—temp up to 75. Toddled
over to see Tom the mail toter by
sitting to rest 5 times. To Young's
for papers. Jimmy Dishman and
family and a family from Ft. Worth
here for a long session. Later come
Dewey for a pleasant session—with
gifts.

12th: In a state of bemused ecstatic bliss.

25th: June fotch Mote in by Curtis place to cabin. A grand time all p.m. visiting Mote while Nell and June gathered plants, flowers, etc. for Hal and others. About 4 p.m., our big party started. Earl Garner came first then Paul and Woody and Dewey. They built a roaring fire below the cabin. Dr. Flickinger fotch Mr. Warren 71. Mote and Nell and June enjoyed these men. Dean Stone came and took pictures. Lee Roberson and Dolores came and windy Earl Franklin, Tom Sawyer and Jeff Breazeale. The wine flowed copiously but temperately. June, Mote and Nell took off just at dusk for Knoxville where all spent the night. The fellows stayed a time as it set in raining and they took to cabin to listen to radio. (Earl F.) Earl Garner had his car in here and took Dr. F., Mr. W. and Tom Sawyer out late in a drizzle.

May 5th: Deliberate, leisurely living is possible perhaps only in solitude.

12th: Perfect weather—glorious here. Toddled over to mailbox with many stops for wind.
The 2 milkmen regaled me a time then Tom Sawyer came with mail and fotch me home up power line. Bless Tom—he is a prince.

14th: A perfect May day. These gorgeous May
days slip by like minutes with not
time enough for my reading, writing
and conversation. Dewey here this
p.m. for delightful conversation.

23rd: Let me not suffer
the
humility,
ignominity
and the
indignity of insanity.

A THREE-LEGGED RACE

May 27, 1970

In his last year or two, life according to Bert had resolved into a three-legged race between cancer, cataracts, and insanity. Cancer was sending out swelling fingers into his body, sapping his strength and energy. Cataracts had greatly clouded the vision of his good eye. Insanity wasn't really in the running, but it balanced the serious contestants and gave rise to a chuckle from his friends.

"Bert, you know insanity is far in the lead and has been most of your years," I remarked.

"Yeh, many have always thought I had my head bored for the simples for living off the beaten path. I haven't lived this way to chuck life, but to live it more abundantly." As we drove past the new West Branch of the Bank of Maryville under construction, he quipped, "The bank and I were born in the same year, 1885, but if it's as wobbly as I am, it's in bad shape. I've always banked there and believe she's growing with great vigor, quite in contrast to my declining state...."

"You know, I would sell my business cheap today."

"What business?"

"The business of living, for I am about lived out."

"What has been your business?"

"My business has been leisure, serving as an observer of man and his follies and as inspector of the universe in general, and in particular, as inspector of the Great Smoky Mountains."

"It has been a labor, or leisure, of love, hasn't it?"

"Oh, that it has, and I shall be perfectly content to just be dead when I die.

"George Santayana wrote, 'There is no cure for birth and death save to enjoy the interval,' and my days have been filled with rapture.

"When Old Fate comes with shears to cut my thread, I want to be in my woods. But now it looks as if the thread will be snipped in the hospital or nursing home.

"It was my clear intent to take the lead pill from that old revolver in my trunk when the end approached. I have contemplated that most seriously and can't explain my reluctance to take that medicine and close out a life, fully lived and now over, except for the final stages now upon me. Euthanasia is justified and will be accepted of necessity in the near future. When one is old and living only to die, the prolonging of death is often cruel and unreasonable.

"The Eskimo custom of sending the old out in the cold when they were past functioning as family members was more humane than our practice of keeping vegetables alive. Society must soon view mercy deaths as fitting and proper for the deathly ill and their families. But we move so slowly to do that which must be done."

Bert was always loquacious, but never on his health. It was on his mind this day, and I encouraged him to talk, touching subjects which had come up in the past and probing to elicit his feelings. Time was short and he was more aware of this than was I. This fact caused him to speak fluently about himself and his feelings at this time. What follows is the essence of what he said on that May morning.

"Life is the jailer for the aged and sick; death is but an angel sent to draw the unwilling bolts and set us free. Lately I have grown tired of living in this clay carcass; it is too much trouble to feed, clothe, and pander to. It was a keen satisfaction and even a delight to watch nature remove me from the living. Death will now be a welcome extinction—oblivion. Ole Shakespeare said, 'Our little life is rounded with a sleep.' I fear death no more than I fear going to sleep each night. Yet, I have gotten a bit impatient because Father Time moves so slowly. I want to get the job done. I have warmed my hands and my heart at the fire of life. The fire burns low, and I'm ready to go.

"The aged seldom fear death, and I have often sat with and ministered to the needs of the dying. Most are unconscious when they go and have no awareness of pain, pending death, or its arrival. It is the youth who fear death. They are too young to accept or to understand it, whereas it is a common occurrence for the old, having witnessed death time and again with friends and family." We arrived at the cabin after driving up the power line across the fields and parked by the old woodshed. He walked with difficulty to the cabin, browsed around and began wrapping a package to mail to Nell, his stepdaughter. After he finished, we went out into the morning sun and Bert continued to reveal his thoughts.

"In the old days, the church bells would give the death toll. Knowing who was seriously ill in the community, we would usually know for whom the bells tolled and would go to the graveyard, lay out all the land a man takes with him, 2' x 6', and dig the grave. In or around 1950, they stopped this neighborly service in Carpenters and began charging $20 to dig a grave. Chet McGhee and I made a pact to save one family the expense of the funeral. The one who remained would dig the grave, buy the coffin, and pay all funeral expenses. We had fun discussing our agreement when we met to pass the time. Around 1959, he was seriously ill. On one of my visits, he said that he had been thinking of our pact and had come to the conclusion that the only way he could win was by dying. He asked to void the agreement. This we did, and he died shortly thereafter.

"Bob Kolsbun and I had agreed in Philadelphia that in the event of a deathly illness on the part of either that the other would help him to take his own life and have the remains cremated and buried without ceremony. Looks like I have need of Bob now to fulfill his part of the bargain.

"I ordered a heart attack to take me but had to settle for cancer. I don't look forward to the indignity of helplessness. I shall greet death exuberantly, with a glad hand. It is my hope to croak before I go nuts, deaf, or blind. The Grim Reaper is a jolly good friend of all the aged sick. I don't share with Hamlet, 'The dread of something after death.'

"The best part of my life has been the last twenty years since I left Curtis. I have had, until recently, excellent health and have walked the mountains and fields as strongly as I did in my youth. I have met all manner of men and enjoyed our conversations. My friendships have increased in depth and in numbers, and my joy in living has only recently diminished. My main regret is that I have 500 years of reading which will remain unread. I shall miss laughing my fool head off at the foibles of mankind. Man is now harnessed to and driven by his technology and machinery. He has become the slave of his own inventions.

"Man is ruled by his emotions rather than his intellect. We should not be too concerned when he fails to respond in a rational way to his problems. This has caused me more anguish than anything. Man will be inundated by the weight of the problems he has created unless his intellect takes over and he puts himself in a better balance with nature. His worst enemy is himself.

"Rachel Carson's *Silent Spring* isn't far in the future unless man curbs his appetites and establishes sound practices for treatment of his small spaceship, Mother Earth, which he has ravished as if her resources were endless. He should treat her like a mother and the source of his life rather than as a common whore to be screwed endlessly and treated shamefully. She should be treated with gentle hands, a loving heart, and deep respect. We are literally born and nurtured by the dust of the earth. Yet, we exploit this speck in space recklessly and tragically. How long will it take man to come to his senses?" We had been seated for some time under a serviceberry tree near the fence below the cabin. Bert sat with his back against the trunk, his legs outstretched, and his feet bare in the sun, wiggling his toes in the leaves. His thin, white hair was unruly, his eyebrows white with a soft sprinkling of pepper. Brown patches of age blotted his tanned, leather face. His clothes were worn and sagging, the collar of his blue shirt was open. The loose, worn trousers had two small ragged tears on the right lower leg and a large tear on the left leg, souvenirs left by briers or snags which had caught as he had traversed his pathway with poor vision.

A wood hen, pileated woodpecker, drummed on an oak deep in the woods. The locusts were singing. A cardinal flew across the yard and settled into its nest in the purple-stalked raspberry bushes. We talked of his hospital stay.

"Ted Flickinger and Bob Mynatt have been mighty good to me. I've never had the highest respect for doctors, but these boys have almost changed my mind. I've asked them to talk to me straight, and I think they have. One told me last week, 'I got good news for you, Bert; you're going to die. Your cancer is all right but your lungs are giving you a problem that we can't lick.'

"You know I've never been billed for the last 18 months of service from them; so several months ago I sent them a signed, blank check and asked them to fill it in for what I owed. The check never came through; so on my last visit I asked about that check. You know what they told me? 'We filled it in for a million dollars and it was returned, marked "insufficient funds".'

"The hospital isn't the best place for a dying man. It's too busy, too many people coming and going. Too many orderlies, too many cleaners, too many visitors. The preachers were busy, too. I don't mind them as occasional callers, but they seem to be driven to have you rest in peace. Yet, I have always rested and worked in peace. If a man isn't ready for death at eighty-four, I don't know what a preacher can do for him. One fellow caught me in a low moment, and when he began questioning me, I answered with some of Mark Twain from *Letters From The Earth*."

"Have you made your peace with God?"

"For the life of me, I've never had the slightest quarrel with Him."

"Have you renounced the Devil?"

"My God, man, I'm in no condition to make enemies of anyone at the moment, much less the Devil.

"Can't the horse pistol do something about those pestering preachers; put a leash on them and hold them to their own flocks?"

I told him that one of the orderlies informed me that it was the first time he had worked in the room of a terminal patient where there was a three-ring circus going on continuously. Bert replied, "I've always wanted to go to hell a whooping. While working one summer in 1902 for the Little River Lumber Company as a lumber scaler, we shipped sound, wormy chestnut to the National Casket Company. Fellows around there would say they wanted to be buried in

190

chestnut, so they could go through hell a poppin'. Chestnut cracks and pops up a storm when it burns, you know.

"I had more visitors than I could handle, and it was fine until I began to tire at night. One evening I was tuckered out and had more folks in than I could stomach. There was a card on the door which said 'only one visitor at a time.' But people won't, or don't, read. There were as many as six in at once. Anyhow, my nephew came in as they flashed the lights, signaling visitors to leave and lights out. I told him to close the door; he did and proceeded to stand by my bed. I told him I meant to get on the other side of it and close it. A man is more cantankerous with his family than with others; which is as it should be, although rough on the family at times."

He was brisk in these irascible moods and didn't like people to ask him how he was.

"My first reaction to such questions was to say none of your damn business, but I refrained most of the time and talked about the weather or some other inane subject."

To one woman he wasn't so delicate but retorted to her question as to how he was, "Terrible, I'm going to die tonight." The poor woman quickly made herself scarce.

One lady had stopped me at the door to his room as she left and asked if I was a friend. I answered in the affirmative, and she said, "I just learned he was sick and can't believe it. He was like a young man in his old age. When my father was on his death bed thirty years ago, Bert nursed him night after night, and we all grew

191

especially close to him. When he goes, it'll be like losing a member of the family. All the people in Carpenters feel that way about him.

"He always sat up with and visited the sick and brought a lot of joy with him and left it when he departed. He was a most unusual man."

The remainder of his life was a rapid decline. His old friend, Robert Kolsbun from Philadelphia, came from his retirement home in Florida. His stay was brief because he found Bert quite ill. Two of the last three weeks were spent at the hospital and the last at Montvale Nursing Home where he was under heavy sedation and asleep much of the time.

The following are some of his comments to me during his last weeks:

"Lonas Clark (long time acquaintance) liked to play his own chin music. He told me that after long study he had come to the conclusion that when he got to heaven there would be no one there but him and God."

"Last time I went to my cabin (around July 10th) I had to tie myself to a tree to keep from flying off, I was so happy."

"Just killing time till time kills me."

"Can't read, can't write, can't think; so I'm in bad shape."

"You've finished your daily chores, have you? I've about finished mine, my life's chores too."

His thread was sheared in the night of August 7, 1970. He died as peacefully as he had lived.

CONCLUSION

Carson Brewer, a friend of Bert's and a staff writer for the Knoxville *News-Sentinel*, wrote of his death on August 9, 1970:

MOUNTAIN SCHOLAR IS GONE; SAGE OF THE SMOKIES DIES; BERT GARNER WAS A 'BUCCOLIC SOPHISTICATE.'

Bert Garner, naturalistic, philosopher and scholar who for years lived alone in the woods in a rustic cabin he built for $87.50 about 1920, is dead.

He died Friday night of cancer, an ailment of which he spoke almost lightly. He was 84.

"I am host to a cancer," he said to friends a year ago, explaining why he couldn't hike as fast or as far as he once did.

But his towering six-foot-four frame still moved along a trail faster than some of his companions. He hiked all over the Great Smokies. He once hiked to Asheville, about 125 miles, in three days.

An amazing blend of the rustic and the sophisticate, Bert Garner was equally at ease with Great Smokies mountaineers and scholars and students from all over the country who came to his cabin in the woods.

Ole Bert: Sage of the Smokies

From the editorial page of the *Maryville-Alcoa Daily Times* of August 10, 1970 appeared:

BERT GARNER WAS WELL-LIKED, ARTICULATE BACKWOODSMAN.

Bert Garner has lived out his full score of years and passed away in a local nursing home over the weekend.

A fully educated, articulate, and well-read backwoods character, Bert lived in a small home with the bare necessities of life. He existed yearly on such a minimum amount of cash that he was the subject of a television show not many years ago.

Bert was not a recluse for having rejected the materialism of modern society in the present sense of the word for he loved to talk to people and he enjoyed their company. He simply preferred to live in his own fashion and sought solitude to read and think.

Bert knew the mountains and delighted in long trips into the heart of the Great Smokies. He often went with other natives, sharing his knowledge of nature and locality with them. The infirmities of his age were never so clear to him than when he had to cease this activity.

The death of Bert Garner will leave a void in many lives although he long was a loner in his private life. His way of life belonged to a bygone era yet some of the philosophical discussions of this man are making more and more sense in a world battered with kooky ideas.

From a long obituary in the *Maryville-Alcoa Daily Times* on August 10, 1970, written by Bert's friend, Dean Stone, the following is extracted:

MOUNTAIN PHILOSOPHER BERT GARNER, 84, IS VICTIM OF CANCER.

A mountain philosopher and lover of the Smokies, he was among the best read residents of the county and had received considerable national publicity because of his love for the simple life.

Typical of some of Bert's philosophy were:

"The wisdom of economy and the dignity of simplicity should be more emphasized in our schools. I have savored the delightful sweets of the simple life.

"Freedom means more than money anytime. Most people never know real freedom. They have become wage slaves.

"To me time is a golden asset. I am never idle. Don't waste time, the precious thing life is made of, working for useless things.

"The pursuit of leisure is an accomplished art. I have the leisure I want to learn and study.

"The accumulation of the world's goods never compensates for loss of tranquility of soul."

Bert had requested Dewey Simpson to notify by letter, after his death, a number of friends and correspondents across the country. There were fifteen prompt replies to this notice, and something of Bert's remarkable capacity for friendship and some evidence of his influence is revealed in the following representative excerpts from five of the letters.

From Bert's host at the Garry Moore Show came: "The news of Bert Garner's death was saddening. I too have lost a good, valued friend whose greatness of character I recognized at our first meeting, when he came to New York to appear on the Gary Moore television show. I can truthfully say that after that exciting meeting, on a bitter cold New Year's Day night, I was a changed man. For the first time I had met a man who not only lived for his ideas but tried to live them simply and naturally and in the process inspired other people to examine themselves and their lifestyles as no orthodox religionist could inspire them to do. He fanned a spark in many, many people. I feel myself to be a better person as a consequence of having known Bert."

Edward E. Warres Jamaica, N. Y. August 16, 1970

From a young man of relatively short acquaintance:

"i received your kind letter the other day relating mr. garner's death. it was forwarded to me by my parents, who knowing of my relationship with bert these past three years, first told me of his death last sunday. i had seen him just this past june and knew he wouldn't have much longer to live. but it is always easier to accept this mentally than emotionally. i miss him very much and shall because to me, too, he was and is a great man, and greater still, a civilized thinking human being. of all the people i have met, he is the only one who contained complete peace about him and communicated this to other people.

"all the times i visited his land, it, like him, emitted a great feeling of peace about it that descended upon one as he walked the path to his cabin. "

bren nichols
new york city
16 august 1970

From a lady friend:

"He meant so much to me as he was a very dear and true friend. During our years of correspondence, his letters brought me much happiness, especially when I was sad and troubled. His letters carried much hope and cheer, and after reading them I always felt better.

"How can I ever forget someone like Bert Garner? I shall never forget him, he was the most wonderful person I ever knew in my life."

Mrs. Angela Rolkowski
Camden, New Jersey
August 16, 1970

From a local girl who had moved away:

"Like you, I feel that I have lost one of the best friends I have ever known. I grew up as a close neighbor of Bert and some of my earliest recollections are of standing in awe of this great man. As I grew older we became very good friends; and I never returned to Maryville to visit my family but that this visit also included a visit to Bert; either that or he would hear that I was home and come to visit me. These visits were a highlight of my trip back to Tennessee; for a nice chat with him was so very enjoyable.

"I had read in the Washington newspaper of his passing away; and felt the obituary very short and insufficient; but on second thought, this was exactly the way Bert would have wished it." Loa Nell Reid Laurel, Md. August 19, 1970

From a correspondent who had never met him:

"Although I was never fortunate enough to meet Bert in person we have been close friends through our letters for 13 years and I considered it one of those rare, once in a lifetime, friendships. His death is a great loss to each of his thousand-fold friends, and also to the world. With the deterioration of mankind and the stupid destruction of this beautiful world we need men like him—but now he is gone. He was the special kind of person one doesn't find anymore and I know that his great wisdom, understanding and compassion, touched some deep chord in everyone he ever met—people from all walks of life—of any age."

Frances R. Pecsi Galesburg, Illinois Aug. 15th, 1970

Bert had donated his body to the University of Tennessee Medical School in Memphis. In October 1971 his ashes were returned for burial. Following is his letter of instructions to the funeral home: "Paradise" R6, Maryville, Tenn. 2-15-1966

McCammon and Ammons Maryville, Tenn.

Distinguished Gentlemen:

This letter to be attached to my donation form you have on file. In case I die in the mountains, or elsewhere, and my body be not immediately found the remains are to be cremated and the ashes turned over to my executor, Earl D. Garner, Maryville, Tenn. The U. T. Medical College Anatomy Dept, wrote me a fine, long letter thanking me for my gift. They say that no cadavers are now used at Knoxville U. T. Hospital but may be later. If a casket must be used either for transportation or cremation, I request that it cost no more than $100.00. One bed sheet is good enough for me to wear, and no cosmetics. I request no festivities, "going away party", flowers, music, singing or braying (praying). If Fred Garner, or anyone else, wishes to shoot one firecracker that's O.K. by me. If you have to take me to your funeral home, I promise to keep my fool mouth shut. I may go to several of your funerals yet.

With all good will and cordiality,
Herbert S. (Bert) Garner

His ashes were buried in Carpenter's Cemetery on October 17, 1971, with family and friends gathered. The service consisted of the following tribute delivered by the author:

We are here to pay our last respects to an unusually refreshing personality. No one can paint an adequate word picture of Ole Bert. There was too much of him to capture with words or with any other form of expression. He was like a vigorous breeze across this countryside, leaving those he visited with renewed spirits.

We can say, without question, that he was the only one of his kind.

His enthusiasm for life never diminished until his last illness. He had the heart and curiosity of a child throughout his eighty-four years. Nothing was too insignificant to capture his interest.

He was a good neighbor, and he was a good friend. His closest friend during his Philadelphia years was Bob Kolsbun, photographer for the *Saturday Evening Post.* In one of his letters to me, Bob wrote, "Of all my years, the hours I spent with "Tennessee" (Ole Bert) were the most precious. Those years together in Philadelphia were the high years of my life."

Bert kept alive the dying art of conversation. He conversed on your level and drew you out on your interests. His fund of information was encyclopedic.

He decided early to live as simply as possible, to keep his mind as well as his house uncluttered. The more he could do without, the better off he was.

He was a questioner and a searcher. "I learned," he said, "that one should not accept without question the ways of institutions, schools, churches, or governments. I believe in order, but order based on reasonable and logical foundations. By accepting without question the ways of the past, we often perpetuate customs which are out of date and completely unsound. We are now going through a revolution which is shaking the very foundation of our society. (This was in May 1970.) We are being forced belatedly to question and restructure our institutions.

Look how they have changed in recent years, and they will continue to change or cease to exist."

He had a flame in his heels, red pepper in his shoes, and wanderlust flowed in his veins. His tall figure, with a light knapsack, walking the roads or across the fields was a familiar sight. He spent many a day with his "foot in his hand," as he called it, visiting across this beautiful, rolling countryside.

Then he would be off to Atlanta, to Chicago, to New York, to California, to Mexico. In any city, his private club was the public library. He talked with people wherever he went to learn what they were thinking, how they were living. He attended churches of every denomination Jewish, Catholic, and Protestant. In 1926, forty-four years before his death, he wrote, "I've rummaged every city from Boston to 'Frisco."

Bert was so self-reliant and insistent on paying his way that it was difficult to give him anything unless it was left in his mailbox. He was of such strict moral character that few could measure up to the code he practiced. He was a self-confident and disciplined individual.

He was his own man. He marched to the tune he heard, and claimed it to be the music of the spheres.

Paraphrasing Whitman:

He lived to be the ruler of life, not a slave.
He met life as a conqueror,
No fumes, no ennui, no complaints.

"Wear the Garment of Life loosely;" he said, "if it binds, rip it." And he ripped the garment of conventionality and lived lustily in his own inimitable fashion.

He loved this land, this people, and these mountains, and he could never stay long away. "The mountains are my altars; the sunrises and sunsets my inspiration."

On death, "I have no more fear of Death than I have of going to sleep at night. Death is as much a part of life as birth." And death was no stranger to him, for he had sat with and attended to the needs of many friends and neighbors in their last hours down through a long parade of years.

"May I rest in death in or not far from the mountains which have been my life," he wrote in Philadelphia. And in this setting he now rests beside his parents whom he held in high regard, and from whom he received that strange mixture of genes which formed the basis for the incomparable character and personality of Herbert S. Garner.

BLOUNT COUNTY FRIENDS OF THE LIBRARY

The Blount County Friends of the Library exists to advance the mission of the Blount County Public Library by providing financial and organizational support.

Vision
The Blount County Friends of the Library will promote the resources, services and needs of the library through advocacy, education and community support. We offer our continued commitment to help make our library the best it can be in serving our community.

Core Belief
Members of the Blount County Friends of the Library share a passion for libraries and a desire to help their library meet the challenges of the day, as well as remain vital far into the future.

Supporting the Library
The primary purpose of a Friend of the Library group is to be of service to the library through the following activities:

- **Money**–Friends of the Library raise funds for projects or acquisitions in excess of the general library budget.
- **Services**–There is no limit to the services that a dedicated volunteer group can provide.
- **Public Relations**–Each Friend is *an advocate* for the library to its community.

- **Community Involvement**–A Friend of the Library group is validation of the public library's importance to its community.
- **Advocacy**–An informed, active citizen lobby provides the public library with its strongest allies.

SOUTHERN APPALACHIAN STUDIES SERIES

This book is part of the Southern Appalachian Studies Series of the Blount County Public Library, as are the following:

Foothills Voices (2017)

FOOTHILLS VOICES (2017)

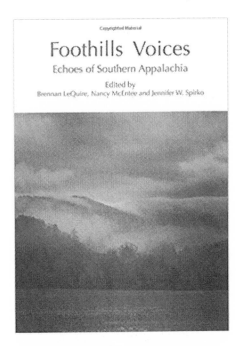

Twelve East Tennessee writers share stories from their own experiences, their families and their communities. In this collection are true accounts of Revolutionary War-era ancestors, Native Americans, civil rights pioneers, coal miners, mill workers, teachers, soldiers, orphans, feuding mountaineers and even a murderer. These writers reveal the rich and varied heritage of Southern Appalachia while giving voice to stories that transcend regional limitations.

Get your copy **today on Amazon** and read these fascinating stories.

Foothills Voices, volume 2 (forthcoming, 2019)

THE ONE I KNEW THE BEST OF ALL
BY FRANCES HODGSON BURNETT

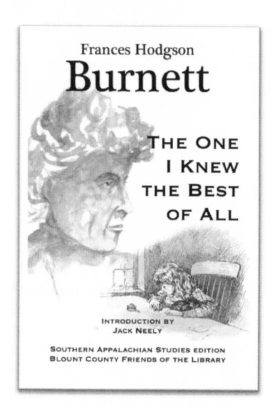

When she was a teenager, author Frances Hodgson Burnett (*Little Lord Fauntleroy, The Secret Garden*) moved with her family from a comfortable existence in Manchester, England, to East Tennessee. It was 1865, and the scars of the American Civil War were still visible, particularly in Knoxville where the Hodgsons located. It was not an easy place for a teenage girl to be.

But Frances made the best of it.

Ole Bert: Sage of the Smokies

As Jack Neely writes in the introduction: "It was an extreme shift for what had been an affluent middle-class big-city family to live in near-frontier conditions, without even enough income to feed themselves well. With a good measure of romanticism, Frances adapted. She had been a fan of the *Leatherstocking Tales* of James Fenimore Cooper, whose frontier adventures were as popular in England as in America. She saw elements of his famous settings in her new home."

It was here, in the shadow of the Great Smoky Mountains, that Frances began her extraordinary writing career. And it was here that she returned, in her mind's vision, to write a remarkable and often overlooked autobiographical novel, *The One I Knew the Best of All.*

The novel is a delightful account of a childhood, protected but full of good stories and small adventures. It is told from the child's point of view and describes the emotions of the Small Person – as Frances coyly refers to herself – as she encounters relatives, friends, adults who would take advantage of her and those who would befriend her. She meets the realities of death and loss and the joys of achievement and friendship. She develops a taste for reading, then for storytelling, and finally for writing

Those who want to know about Frances and how she began her long and wildly successful writing career need to read this book. Those who want insights about how a bright and innocent child sees the world and develops the wherewithal to face it should study this book.

Those who simply want a good story -- one that your children could read or you could read to them -- should obtain this book and put it in an honored place in your library. Nothing else like it exists

This book is a part of the Southern Appalachian Studies Editions, published by the Blount County Friends of the Library in Maryville, Tennessee. The purpose of the series is to bring out new editions of work by writers who have connections to East Tennessee.

38968340R00137

Made in the USA
Middletown, DE
15 March 2019